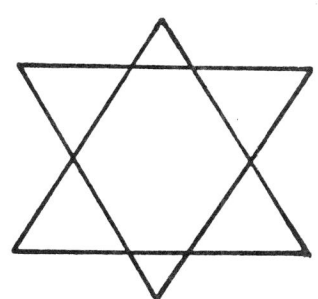

DEFINING THE ROLE OF THE NON-JEW IN THE SYNAGOGUE:

A Resource for Congregations

Commission on Reform Jewish Outreach
of the Union of American Hebrew Congregations
and the Central Conference of American Rabbis

Copyright © 1990, Union of American Hebrew Congregations
Manufactured in the United States of America
1 2 3 4 5 6 7 8 9

כָּל־מַחֲלֹקֶת שֶׁהִיא לְשֵׁם שָׁמַיִם סוֹפָהּ לְהִתְקַיֵּם

Every controversy conducted for God's sake
will in the end prove fruitful.

Pirke Avot 5:20

Through faith man experiences the meaning of the world;
through action he is to give to it a meaning.

Leo Baeck

This Resource is dedicated to
LOTTIE AND WILLIAM DANIEL
who have faith in the future of the Jewish people
and whose actions serve to ensure our survival

Table of Contents

	Page
Preface	1
Acknowledgements	2
To the Rabbi and Temple President	5

Section One: Exercises 13

    Exercise I: Focusing Exercise on Clarifying Personal Positions 15

    Exercise II: Temple Purposes 17

    Exercise III: What's Jewish about Jewish Leadership?   20

    Exercise IV: A Letter from an Intermarried Woman . 22

    Exercise V: Scenarios and Strategies . . . 26

    Exercise VI: The Jewish Survival Game . . . 29

Section Two: Guidance from our Tradition

    I.   Exploring Jewish Prayer and Ritual . . . 34

    II.   The Role of the Non-Jew in the Synagogue: Setting the Discussion in Context . . . 42

    III.   Guidance from Our Sources: Selected Reform Responsa 45

Section Three: Essays

    "Non-Jews and Jewish Life Cycle Liturgy"
        by Rabbi Lawrence Hoffman 65

    "Some Comments on Lawrence Hoffman's Essay"
        by Rabbi W. Gunther Plaut 83

    "Jewish Life-Cycle Liturgy and Non-Jews"
        by Rabbi Joseph B. Glaser 87

    "Non-Jews at Jewish Celebrations"
        by Rabbi Harvey J. Fields 89

    "The Role of the Non-Jewish Parent in Synagogue Life-Cycle Ceremonies: A Rabbi's Reflections"
        by Rabbi Lawrence Mahrer 92

	Page
"The Role of the Non-Jew and the Temple Constitution" by Rabbi Sally Preisand	100

Section Four: Applying What We Have Learned
Making Congregational Policy 109

Appendices

I.	Membership and Religious Background: Excerpts from Congregational Membership Forms	116
II.	UAHC Affiliates: Guidelines Regarding Non-Jewish Members	122
III.	Outreach - Related Reform Responsa: A Reference Guide	125
IV.	What is Outreach?	128
V.	Suggested Reading	134
VI.	Regional Outreach Staff	136

Preface

Reform Judaism's Outreach program is predicated on the assumption that intermarriage will remain a reality of American Jewish life, that, far from diminishing, the rate of intermarriage is likely to increase, and that, in consequence, the better part of wisdom is not to reject the intermarried, but rather to love them all the more, to do everything we humanly can to draw them closer to us, and to involve them in Jewish life.

The synagogue embraces the non-Jewish mates of our children. We invite them to worship with us, to learn about Judaism, to share the Jewish life-cycle celebrations of their family members, and to participate in the temple's work should they choose to do so.

The role of the non-Jew in the synagogue, however, requires clarification; its bounds must be defined. This resource is designed to help the lay and professional leaders of our congregations to deal sensitively with the issue of non-Jews in our synagogues while preserving the integrity of Judaism.

Hopefully this resource will advance the goal of all our Outreach striving: to bring non-Jews bound to us by marriage to Judaism, or to make certain that the children issuing from these marriages, our children's children, and their children in turn -- l'dor vador -- will, in fact, be reared as Jews and share the destiny of this people Israel.

> Rabbi Alexander M. Schindler
> President
> Union of American Hebrew Congregations

Acknowledgements

UAHC-CCAR Commission on Reform Jewish Outreach

Melvin Merians, *Chairman*
Rabbi Leslie Gutterman, *Co-Chairman*
Lydia Kukoff, *Director and Executive Editor*
Rabbi Nina J. Mizrahi, *Editor*
Dru Greenwood, *Associate Director and Co-Editor*
Sherri Alper, *Consultant for Special Programming*
Rabbi Renni Altman, *Director, Task Force on the Unaffiliated*

Regional Outreach Staff

Canadian Council, Jessie Caryll
Great Lakes Council/Chicago Federation, Mimi Dunitz
Mid-Atlantic Council, Elizabeth Farquhar
Midwest Council, Marsha Luhrs
New Jersey/West Hudson Valley Council, Kathryn Kahn
New York Federation of Reform Synagogues, Ellyn Geller
Northeast Council, Paula Brody
Northeast Lakes Council, Nancy Gad-Harf
Northern California Council/Pacific Northwest Council, Lisa Cohen Bennett
Pacific Southwest Council, Arlene Chernow
Pennsylvania Council/Philadelphia Federation, Linda Steigman
Southeast Council/South Florida Federation, Rabbi Rachel Hertzman
Southwest Council, Debby Stein

Administrative Staff: Muriel Finn, Gail Sussnow
Cover Design: Rayleen Buys, Helayne Friedland

* * *

We express special gratitude to these contributors:
Sherri Alper, A.C.S.W., M.S.W.
Rabbi Lester Bronstein
Rabbi Harvey Fields
Rabbi Joseph Glaser
Rabbi Lawrence Hoffman
Rabbi Lawrence Mahrer
Rabbi W. Gunther Plaut

We would like to express our appreciation to those congregations whose experiences in exploring congregational policy created the foundation for this resource.

We would also like to thank all those who served as readers and who offered many valuable insights which enriched this documents.

UAHC-CCAR Commission on Reform Jewish Outreach

Bernice Altshuler
Patricia Anixter
David Belin
Robert Benjamin, Jr.
Carol Beyer
Rabbi Lee Bycel
Harriet Carson
Rabbi Paul Citrin
Dr. Norman Cohen
Donna Corby
William Daniel
Rabbi Harry Danziger
Harry Davidson
Sue Eckstein
Rabbi Kenneth Ehrlich
Carl Feldman
Rabbi Steven Foster
Dianne Friedman
Toni Golbus
Ernest Grunebaum
Lois Gutman
Susan Halpert
Rabbi Stephen Hart
Dr. Robert Hess
Isabelle Horne
Richard Imershein
Rabbi Walter Jacob
Janet Kahn
Lee Kahn-Goldfarb
Fern Kamen
Roger Karlebach
Dr. Ronald Kaye
Mary Lynn Kotz
Madeleine Lebedow

Dr. Richard Lewis
Liz Linkon
Stanley Loeb
Madeleine Kelly Lubar
Rabbi Eugene Mihaly
Jacques Morris
Rabbi Frank Muller
Theodore M. Pailet
Judy Picus
Colleen Rabin
Constance Reiter
Rabbi Jeffrey Salkin
Stan Sandler
Sheila Saunders
Henry Seiff
Bev Shafran
Cantor Raymond Smolover
Dr. Robert Stier
Ernest Stern
Susie Teschner
Jerry Tilles
David Toomin
Paul Uhlmann, Jr.

Ex-Officio Members

Rabbi Howard I. Bogot
Rabbi Joseph Glaser
Allan B. Goldman
Rabbi Samuel E. Karff
Rabbi Alexander M. Schindler
Rabbi Mark Dov Shapiro
Rabbi Daniel B. Syme
Rabbi Mark L. Winer

To the Rabbi and Temple President:

Congregations throughout North America have begun examining the impact that the changing demography of the American Jewish community will have on the synagogue. It is a fact of life that increasing numbers of intermarried couples are choosing to join us. As these couples begin to strengthen their ties with the Jewish community, we are challenged to define the role of the non-Jew in the synagogue. It is crucial that congregations take a <u>proactive</u>, rather than reactive, approach to this definition process. Doing so can prevent some potentially painful and damaging situations. Helping your congregational leadership and your congregation to understand the balance between preserving the integrity of Judaism and responding sensitively to the human needs of those involved is vital to our future.

Our success in achieving this balance is dependent on the extent to which lay and professional leadership are able to work together, learn from one another and create a shared vision for the future of American Judaism. The "Guidelines for Rabbinical-Congregational Relationships," which is jointly published by the Union of American Hebrew Congregations and the Central Conference of American Rabbis, describes the partnership of the congregational leadership and the Rabbi as follows:

> A congregation is best served when its lay and rabbinic leadership consider themselves partners in carrying on the sacred functions of the synagogue. Certainly the lay leadership and the rabbi should interact on all levels of congregational activity. The officers, board, congregational committees, and the rabbi should work closely together: the lay leadership always calling upon the rabbi for expert advice, based upon scholarship and experience; the rabbi respecting the judgment, sensitivity, and commitment of the leadership (p.3).

The following two scenarios provide a sense of the issues which challenge our congregations:

* Tom Elkins has been a faithful supporter of the Temple for fifteen years. He was married by the Temple's rabbi, has been involved in various activities, attends services with his family, and has become a respected presence in the temple. Although Tom has never converted because of his parents who live nearby, he shares his wife's and daughter's Judaism in every way. The Elkins' daughter will become a Bat Mitzvah within six months, and the family has asked that Tom participate fully in the event...

* Temple Beth David's Board of Trustees has decided to consider whether or not non-Jews may become Board members. There are a number of intermarried couples who are very active in the congregation, with many non-Jewish

spouses who work hard to organize and support various activities. In the normal sequence of congregational life, if they were Jewish, they would be asked to join the Board. Several Board members believe that non-Jewish partners should be eligible for Board positions, provided they have demonstrated a commitment to the congregation and a willingness to work. Others feel that only Jews should make policy decisions for the congregation and the community, including that of engaging the congregation's new rabbi next year....

These and other issues discussed in this resource may not yet have arisen in your congregation, but the chances are that, at some point, they will. The best way to deal with these issues is to face them head on <u>before</u> there is a problem.

Whether the status of non-Jews in the synagogue is considered before a difficult situation arises or in response to one, the setting of such standards is likely to cause a period of disruption in the temple family. Members are likely to have strong opinions either way, and feelings may include righteous indignation, anger, betrayal, and hurt. The difficulties are twofold: there is little precedent for policy in this area, and the subject of intermarriage (and thus, the role of the non-Jew in the synagogue) is an emotionally-charged topic. For a period of time, there may seem to be much heat and little light.

With the prospect of such pain in mind and with the old ways of doing things firmly entrenched, many congregations are wary of tackling what may seem, at the outset, to be such an overwhelming challenge. The material gathered in this resource is intended to shed light through education about various issues that arise, and to dissipate heat through acknowledgement of the feelings of each "side." The goals are relatively simple:

* To help non-Jews and their Jewish partners understand the concerns of the Temple for its boundaries, and

* To help Jews understand the perspective of non-Jews who may choose to deepen their involvement in the life of the temple, but who, for whatever reason, do not currently choose to convert.

Without a strong sense of identity and mission, no institution can function effectively in relation to those it serves. While vague policies may seem to offend no one, they neither serve the reality of the present-day synagogue nor ensure its future.

<u>DEFINING THE ISSUES</u>

The role of non-Jews in the synagogue should be considered in relation to three separate areas of synagogue life: **membership**, **governance/leadership**, and **ritual**.

Membership concerns are generally related to who may join the synagogue. These concerns touch on such questions as:

* What is the mission of the synagogue?

* How can this mission best be promoted?

* Can a non-Jew be a member of a synagogue?

* If so, is s/he entitled to the same rights and privileges as a Jewish member?

* Is it appropriate to establish different categories of membership?

Governance/leadership issues refer to the decision-making process in congregations. The following questions may be raised by congregations:

* How are Jewish values reflected in the leadership of the congregation?

* To what extent are the values expressed by the leadership uniquely Jewish?

* Are non-Jews permitted to chair committees? Auxiliary organizations? To become Board members? Officers of the congregation?

* What is the basis for determining the involvement of non-Jews in the governance and leadership of the temple?

Ritual issues usually revolve around life cycle events and involvement in public prayer. Questions which arise include:

* May a non-Jewish parent sit on the <u>bimah</u> during a Bar/Bat Mitzvah ceremony?

* Must one be Jewish to bless the Shabbat candles during services or read the translation of the <u>Haftarah</u>?

* May a non-Jew participate in the Torah service?

* May a non-Jew lead the congregation in worship?

* How can a non-Jewish parent most appropriately express publicly his/her support for his/her child's Jewish upbringing and formal education?

* What is the basis for decision-making about the involvement of the non-Jew in public Jewish ritual practice?

This resource is intended for use as a guide to enable you to assess carefully your current policies and chart your future. <u>It should not be viewed as an attempt to dictate specific policy</u>. It provides an overview of issues which arise as a result of seeking to define the role of the non-Jew in the synagogue. Specific exercises to trigger and guide group discussion, discussions of various relevant Jewish texts and concepts, and selected essays will enable you to explore the role of non-Jews in your congregation. Though our goal is to help congregations develop policy in this area, this resource is not intended as an answer book, but rather as a guide to the <u>process</u> of decision-making. The material presented was developed by rabbis and lay leaders who have engaged in an exploration of these issues. A broad spectrum of opinions and decisions are expressed in order to provide the reader with a sense of how the issues might be dealt with.

TIPS FOR PLANNING

1. Lay the groundwork for presenting the issue to the congregation by instituting workshops on exploring and reinforcing Reform Jewish identity. Use every opportunity to publicize the campaign, including the following: the rabbi's column in the temple bulletin, adult education classes, sermons, workshops and discussion groups for Sisterhood, Brotherhood, Youth Group, etc.

2. Some intermarried couples may be fearful of the possibility of a change in their status at the temple. It is important for these couples to feel that their concerns have been heard and to understand the reasons for the decisions that are being made. With these goals in mind, invite intermarried couples to meet with the rabbi, a member of the the Ritual Committee, or a Board member in an informal setting. "Exploring Jewish Prayer and Ritual" in <u>Section Two</u> may be helpful in enabling intermarried couples to explore issues relating to Jewish prayer and ritual.

3. When the congregation is seeking to define the role of the non-Jew in the life of the synagogue, discussion often begins by addressing issues of ritual involvement. Such issues may be defined more concretely than membership or leadership/governance. Once there is acceptance of distinctions between Jewish and non-Jewish participation, move on to discuss membership and governance.

4. Begin discussion with your Board and committee members by using exercises which enable participants to focus on the issues to be discussed. The exercises in this resource will enable participants to explore these challenging issues in a positive and productive way (see <u>Section Two</u>). Careful consideration should be given to the choice of facilitators.

The facilitator may be the rabbi, temple leader or regional Outreach coordinator or Committee chair, or other similar person who has good group skills and is well-versed in these issues.

5. Remember that providing an educational component will ground your discussion. Suggest using the essays and discussion questions which appear in <u>Sections Two and Three</u> of this guide. Try to begin each meeting or program with a <u>devar torah</u> which touches on some of the issues you plan to discuss.

6. To be able to carry out your policy and to avoid embarrassment, you will need to know who is and is not Jewish in your congregation. While revamping your membership form will help with new members, you will probably need to survey current congregants. Consider whether a personal contact rather than a mailed survey might be possible in your setting. Excerpts from selected congregational membership forms on religious background are included in <u>Appendix I</u>.

7. Your membership materials and Membership Committee members should reflect in a positive manner the rights and privileges of non-Jewish family members. Provide a training session to sensitize the membership committee to these issues. Be sure that the temple office staff has been given orientation about these issues as well.

8. It is always better to address the role of the non-Jew <u>proactively</u> rather than reactively. The issue is best handled before there is a crisis.

9. Discuss the use of terminology. The metaphors of "resident alien" (<u>ger toshav</u>) and "citizen of a country" may be useful in explaining the distinctions. While both share many privileges and responsibilities in our country (freedom to live, work, etc.), citizenship confers additional rights and responsibilities. There is a process for becoming a citizen, just as there is a process for becoming a Jew.

10. Jews-by-Birth and Jews-by-Choice are Jews and enjoy the same rights and privileges. In practice, we should encourage our congregants to use the designation "Jew" for Jews-by-Choice. For the sake of discussion, however, when exploring issues relating to conversion and intermarriage, it is sometimes necessary to make a distinction.

11. Before implementing policy, be certain to provide your congregational leadership, working closely with the rabbi, with enough time to process the issue before discussing it more broadly within the congregation. Discussion should allow for representation of all approaches to the various issues raised.

12. One way of welcoming non-Jews into the congregation is to familiarize them with the way in which the Jewish community operates and to acquaint them with the ways in which the synagogue helps families live Jewishly.

13. The UAHC-CCAR Commission on Reform Jewish Outreach has published an entire library of resource books which will be useful in helping your congregation to develop its congregational Outreach program.

14. Do not hesitate to ask for help from your regional Outreach coordinator or regional director. Talking with other congregations about how they have dealt with similar issues may be helpful as well.

Using this Resource

The exercises in <u>Section One</u> are intended to enable those who are in the process of seeking to define the role of the non-Jew in the synagogue to begin to clarify their own feelings about specific types of involvement. They provide opportunties for Jewish values clarification, exploring the purpose of the temple and defining the role of temple leadership. The study materials in <u>Section Two</u> allow decision-makers to gain insights from traditional and modern texts. Together, <u>Sections One</u> and <u>Two</u> will help prepare participants to grapple with the challenge of articulating a congregational policy which reflects sensitivity to the needs of its members and those involved in the life of the congregation while maintaining the integrity of Judaism.

The essays in <u>Section Three</u> reflect a broad range of experiences and opinions expressed by several rabbis. Each essay is followed by discussion questions and provides much food for thought. These essays can be used as background reading or as a supplement to the focusing exercises.

The material in <u>Section Four</u> is designed to apply what has been learned to congregational policy. Examples of constitutional changes made by congregations are provided. Because making informed choices is the hallmark of Reform Judaism, it is best to explore issues regarding membership, governance/ leadership and ritual prior to tackling policy changes.

SECTION ONE

EXERCISES

The initial challenge is to determine what makes us comfortable or uncomfortable with regard to the involvement of intermarried families in our congregations and to understand why. The exercises in <u>Section One</u> will pave the way for the next step: moving from personal feelings to the establishment of a policy which operationalizes the position the congregation has formally chosen to take so decisions should reflect a process of study and examination. The goal is to preserve the integrity of Judaism while reaching out to those who choose to associate themselves with the Jewish community.

The following "Thought Questions" can be used as an opening exercise, or can be distributed in advance as a means of helping participants begin to articulate some of the issues which will be discussed.

THOUGHT QUESTIONS

For each question, circle "comfortable" or "uncomfortable," whichever applies to the way you feel.

___

1. I am comfortable/uncomfortable when non-Jews are temple members.

2. I am comfortable/uncomfortable when non-Jews are members of temple committees.

3. I am comfortable/uncomfortable when non-Jews chair the ritual committee.

4. I am comfortable/uncomfortable when non-Jews serve on the temple Board.

5. I am comfortable/uncomfortable when non-Jews serve as Sisterhood/Brotherhood president.

6. I am comfortable/uncomfortable when non-Jews serve as temple president.

7. I am comfortable/uncomfortable when non-Jews are members of the temple youth group.

8. I am comfortable/uncomfortable when non-Jews serve as youth group president.

9. I am comfortable/uncomfortable when non-Jews sit on the bimah.

10. I am comfortable/uncomfortable when non-Jews bless Shabbat candles or recite kiddush in the synagogue.

11. I am comfortable/uncomfortable when non-Jews recite blessings in the synagogue.

12. I am comfortable/uncomfortable when non-Jews have an aliyah.

13. I am comfortable/uncomfortable when non-Jews pass the Torah from generation to generation.

14. I am comfortable/uncomfortable when non-Jews carry the Torah for a hakafah.

15. It is/ is not appropriate to read the names of non-Jews for kaddish.

EXERCISE I

FOCUSING EXERCISE ON CLARIFYING PERSONAL POSITIONS

Objective:

To help participants examine their own values and opinions

Target Audience:

Congregational leadership and/or adult discussion group

Time Required:

30-40 minutes

Materials Needed:

A copy of the questionnaire for each participant, pens/pencils

Instructions for the Facilitator:

The attached questionnaire is intended for use as you begin discussion on clarifying the role of the non-Jew in the synagogue.

Distribute copies of the questionnaire to all participants and allow 5-10 minutes for completion. When everyone has finished, begin discussion by asking what the experience of the exercise was like. Were there any statements that seemed particularly problematic? Did participants tend to change their minds about specific statements? Did they circle numbers indicating very strong opinions (numbers 1 and 5), or did they frequently respond in the middle range? Did any of the statements seem outrageous?

When you have allowed time for discussion, conclude the exercise by noting areas of agreement and/or disagreement.

Note: Suggested follow-up to this Focusing Exercise is in Section Two, "The Role of the Non-Jew in the Synagogue: Setting the Discussion in Context."

QUESTIONNAIRE

Please indicate your degree of agreement (1) or disagreement (5) with each of the following statements:

1. An unconverted parent is capable of nurturing Jewish life.

    1   2   3   4   5
    agreement   ------------------------> disagreement

2. Family life in a Jewish home in which one partner has not converted to Judaism is basically the same as in a home in which both partners are Jewish.

    1   2   3   4   5

3. A non-Jew should not be permitted to chair a congregational committee.

    1   2   3   4   5

4. A non-Jew should be able to participate fully in Jewish life-cycle events involving his/her family.

    1   2   3   4   5

5. The role of non-Jews in the synagogue should be addressed on a case-by-case basis since all people are different.

    1   2   3   4   5

6. People should not raise the issue of conversion with non-Jews since it is a very personal matter.

    1   2   3   4   5

7. Non-Jews should not be singled out in any way so long as they are willing to be members and pay dues.

    1   2   3   4   5

8. There are certain things about being Jewish that non-Jews cannot understand.

    1   2   3   4   5

9. There are certain things about being Jewish that even Jews-by-Choice cannot understand.

    1   2   3   4   5

EXERCISE II

TEMPLE PURPOSES

Objectives:

1. To provide participants with an opportunity to consider the variety of reasons for the existence of the synagogue

2. To further participants' understanding of the role of the synagogue within both the Jewish and secular communities

3. To enable participants to consider how the mission of the synagogue can best be promoted

Target Audience:

Congregational leadership (Board of Trustees, Brotherhood and Sisterhood Boards, Executive Committee, etc.)

Time Required:

One hour

Materials Needed:

Copy of the "Temple Purposes" handout for each participant, blackboard or large newsprint pad, chalk, markers, pens/pencils

Instructions for the Facilitator:

The facilitator provides each participant with a copy of the handout which can be found at the end of this exercise.

The facilitator begins by noting that the three temple purposes listed are general goals, found in the literature of the Reform movement. The sub-headings have been identified by leaders in many Reform congregations and, while not "official policy," represent common contemporary Reform Jewish perspectives. They are not listed in any priority order.

If the group is relatively small (8-16 participants), the exercise may be done without sub-grouping. Groups larger than 16 should be broken down into smaller discussion groups. When sub-grouping, follow the same instructions, but ask each sub-group to appoint someone who will chair the group and report back when the larger group reconvenes.

The facilitator proceeds as follows:

1. Ask participants individually to identify two or three temple purposes they consider <u>most</u> important for the congregation at this time and two or three purposes they consider <u>least</u> important for the congregation at this time.

2. Ask the group to try to come to a consensus on the most important and least important purposes. Discuss the reasons for their choices.

3. List the three most important purposes of the temple for the near future on a blackboard or a large pad.

4. Ask the group to describe ways that the top three purposes of the temple are currently implemented. What ideas does the group have about how these purposes might be promoted more effectively in the future? Who is responsible - professional staff? congregational leadership? general membership?

5. Ask the group to describe five attributes necessary or desirable in those who could most effectively promote the goals that have been identified. (Common answers include: Jewish knowledge, willingness to work, financial support, positive regard by other temple members, respect in the community.)

6. Finally, ask participants to consider whether being Jewish is a prerequisite for promoting the purposes identified. (The facilitator should be certain to remind participants that "Jewish" includes <u>both</u> Jews-by-Birth and Jews-by-Choice.) What does "being Jewish" mean? (Knowledgeable? Active? etc.) Must the leadership be Jewish? Why/why not? Is there a role for non-Jews in promoting the purposes described? (Specify).

NOTE: This exercise is adapted from one created by Allan Yasgur for the UAHC - CCAR Department of Synagogue Management Leadership Development Program.

Purposes of the Temple

A synagogue is:

1. **A HOUSE OF WORSHIP**, providing religious services in the temple and promoting religious observance in the home.

    * A PLACE FOR LIFE CYCLE EVENTS, including baby namings, B'nai Mitzvah, weddings, funerals, etc.

2. **A HOUSE OF STUDY**, a resource for Jewish education for all ages.

    * A JEWISH CULTURAL CENTER to promote Jewish music, drama, dance, and literature.

    * A CENTER FOR ETHICS AND VALUES for living in accordance with the tenets of Jewish tradition.

    * A SOCIAL ACTION CENTER for learning about and acting on social issues.

    * A LEARNING CENTER for formal and informal Jewish experiences.

3. **A HOUSE OF ASSEMBLY** for meetings of the congregation and the community which promote general social and Jewish welfare.

    * A SUPPORT SYSTEM for making and promoting friendships, performing mitzvot, and meeting the psychological and social needs for belonging, self-worth, and recognition.

    * A PART OF THE JEWISH COMMUNITY on local, regional, national and international levels. (Examples: UJA, local Jewish charities, Soviet Jewry, Israel, etc.)

    * A SERVICE AGENCY for individuals with special needs, including singles, the elderly, single parents, Soviet immigrants, etc.

EXERCISE III

WHAT'S JEWISH ABOUT JEWISH LEADERSHIP?

Objectives:

1. To enable participants to consider how Jewish values are reflected in their own leadership roles in the congregation

2. To provide an opportunity for participants to understand the value-base of others in leadership roles in the congregation

3. To consider which values are uniquely Jewish

4. To consider how non-Jews may or may not understand and/or share the values as listed

Target Audience:

Congregational leadership (Board of Trustees, Sisterhood and Brotherhood Boards, Executive Committee, etc.)

Time Required:

One hour

Materials Needed:

Blackboard or large newsprint pad, chalk or markers, paper, pens/pencils

Instructions for the Facilitator:

If the group is relatively small (8-16), this exercise may be done without sub-grouping. Groups larger than 16 should be broken down into smaller discussion groups. Follow the same instructions, but ask each group to appoint someone who will be responsible for the group process and will report the results when the larger group reconvenes. Ask the group to brainstorm a list of Jewish values. Write them on the blackboard or a large pad. Some examples of values may include:

Promoting Jewish leadership	Belief in God
Preservation of our history	K'lal Yisrael
Welfare of the Jewish Community	Worship
Serving as "a light to the nations"	Israel
Passing on our heritage to future generations	Tzedakah
Perpetuating a Shabbat and the holidays	
Enhancing the Jewishness of homes	

Ask each member of the group to write on a piece of paper one Jewish value s/he exhibits when assuming a leadership role in the Temple. Record the answers on a large pad or blackboard, noting any duplication of responses. Lead a discussion, with special attention to the following:

1. Are you usually aware of the Jewish value you identified, or those identified by others, in your work on behalf of the congregation? Were any of these values a surprise to you?

2. Are the values listed consistent with a historical perspective on Jewish leadership? (i.e. Jewish leaders are always expected to be role models in giving <u>tzedakah</u>, in studying, in acting ethically. Involve your rabbi in discussion.)

3. Do all Jews share the same values? (For example, must all Jews believe in God to be in leadership positions in our congregation and community?)

4. How many of the values listed are exclusively or specifically Jewish?

5. What can be done to heighten our awareness of the ways that we "operationalize" Jewish values in our work on behalf of the congregation?

6. The facilitator summarizes the discussion to this point, highlighting values which participants have defined as specifically Jewish and noting differences of opinion. It is important to note that in our day-to-day roles in the congregation, it is easy to lose sight of the very strong value-base that informs and inspires our work.

7. Finally, the facilitator asks the group: what implications does our discussion have regarding the role of non-Jews in the Temple? Can non-Jews understand how these values operate within the congregation? Do they need <u>historical</u> background (see question #2) to understand them? Is <u>religious</u> background required? Is an understanding of Judaism as a culture or civilization necessary?

8. The facilitator closes the exercise by asking the group to describe what has been clarified in the course of discussion and to specify any areas still needing further attention.

NOTE: This exercise is adapted from leadership training materials designed by the Task Force on Leadership Development of the UAHC/CCAR Commission on Synagogue Management (revised 1987).

EXERCISE IV

A LETTER FROM AN INTERMARRIED WOMAN

Objective:

To sensitize participants to possible perspectives and feelings of interfaith couples in relation to the role of the non-Jew in the synagogue

Target Audience:

Congregational leadership and/or adult discussion groups

Time Required:

30-45 minutes

Materials Needed:

A copy of the following letter for each participant

Instructions for the Facilitator:

Hand out copies of the following letter to each participant, asking for a volunteer to read it aloud. Lead a discussion, using the discussion questions at the end of the letter as a guide.

A Letter from an Intermarried Woman

Dear Rabbi,

I hope that you will understand why I need to write this letter and express what I'm feeling to you. As you know, it has been a confusing few weeks.

When I came to you initially to talk about Jim's role at Beth Am, I hoped that there would be some clear guidelines--from you, from the Reform movement, from somewhere. I have always known that the Jewish community couldn't sanction our marriage, but I guess I hoped that if we embraced the community strongly enough, they would embrace us fully in return. I guess I shouldn't be surprised by the uncomfortable and half-hearted response we have received. I know enough Jewish history to understand, and your explanation to me was helpful. Intellectually, I _do_ understand. Emotionally, it's still painful.

I think you know how very committed Jim has been to supporting the Judaism of our family in every way possible. He has, after all, given the community our children--no small gift under any circumstances, but a very large gift if you consider his strict Catholic upbringing and his loyalty to his family. He loves his family very much, and I think there is not a single day that goes by when he isn't reminded of the loss they feel because he did not marry someone who is Catholic. Although his own commitment to Catholicism was lost long ago, I know that is not easy for him to accept that our children are different from him in a very fundamental way--and still support the cause of that difference.

I know that you and others at temple probably wonder why he has never converted. He has, after all, attended services more often than ninety percent of the congregation, been the first to volunteer when a lot of the scut work has needed to be done, and has seemed to celebrate the seasons of our Jewish lives so joyfully with us. He has given his money, his time, his children. He has not been able to give what many most want of him: himself.

I think you know that Jim's mother has been a devout Catholic her whole life. Our marriage was probably even more distressing to her than it was to my parents. Jim said that explaining to her that Daniel would have a _brit milah_ instead of a baptism was the hardest thing he has ever done. It would be easier if we did not love her, but we do. Jim feels that were he to convert, she would feel she has lost everything. That may seem overdramatic to you, but it is a reality that we live with every day.

When his mother dies, will he become Jewish then? I don't know. In my heart, I don't think so. He is not religious in any kind of theological sense. Although he is very knowledgeable about Jewish history, he doesn't believe in God. That probably surprises you -

he doesn't talk about that around temple. I know many Jews who are atheists, but that would never be accepted in a convert. The double standard still exists.

But belief in God is hardly the issue. (Funny, isn't it, how all this is related...) The purpose of this letter was to explain some things that might help you to understand Jim -- and our family -- a little better. And there is another agenda, too. You said in your Rosh Hashanah sermon that Reform Judaism has always adapted to change and tried to consider Judaism in relation to contemporary society. Well, it feels self-centered to say, but I believe how congregations respond to the Jims in our midst will, in many ways, determine our future.

"So what does she want?" you're probably asking. I'm not sure. I know I don't want you or the congregation to compromise Jewish values, and Jim would not want that either. But there must be a better way not to close doors. I know that Jim will hang in there, no matter how temple policy gets worked out, but it is my own commitment I'm worried about. We have to find room for people who love us enough to have given so much.

I hope that there will be ways that Jim can be made to feel welcome, without strings attached. I hope that people will appreciate his talents and continue to use them. I hope that there will be an important role (and not just a token prayer or two) for him at Melanie's bat mitzvah. I hope that people will talk with Jim about the decisions he's made and what he would like from the congregation in return.

Please use this letter in whatever way might be helpful. It's time to talk about these things and to do something about them.

At B'nai Mitzvah ceremonies there is a very moving moment when the Torah is passed from one generation to another. I hope that when it is our turn that the congregation will understand that, in a different way, Jim has had as profound a role as I have in the passing.

Sincerely,

Helen

DISCUSSION QUESTIONS

1. Helen describes the Jewish community's response to her marriage as "uncomfortable and half-hearted." From your perspective, is her description accurate?

2. Helen says that she knows enough Jewish history to understand the community's response. What does she mean?

3. Why might someone like Jim agree to raise his children as Jews and be supportive of Judaism?

4. What obligations do intermarried families have to the Jewish community? What obligations does the Jewish community have to them?

5. What is your own emotional reaction to this family?

6. If you were the rabbi, how would you respond to Helen?

7. It is extremely important for the rabbi, temple staff and lay leadership to demonstrate sensitivity to the needs of intermarried families in the congregation. How can this support and sensitivity be cultivated and demonstrated?

8. Can Jim's passing of the Torah be justified?

EXERCISE V

SCENARIOS AND STRATEGIES

Objective:

To provide participants with an opportunity to understand the range of issues that arise in relation to the role of the non-Jew in the synagogue

Target Audience:

Congregational leadership and/or adult discussion groups

Time Required:

One to one and one-half hours

Materials Needed:

A copy of the scenarios for each participant, blackboard and chalk or large newsprint pad and markers

Instructions for the Facilitator:

Distribute copies of one scenario at a time. Ask for a volunteer to read it to the group. Facilitate discussion. You may use the scenarios in any sequence you choose. It is suggested that all three be used so that participants have a broader understanding of the many issues involved. At the end of the time allotted, the facilitator should summarize by noting:

1) the range of issues raised in discussion
2) the emotional response of the group
3) the relevance of issues raised in the scenarios to your own congregation.

SCENARIO A

PARTICIPATION OF NON-JEWISH RELATIVES IN JEWISH RITUALS

Tommy, a 6th grade student in your religious school, is working toward his bar mitzvah. His mother, a practicing Catholic, consults you about the ceremony and the role she and Tommy's dad will play. It is customary in your synagogue for the parents to hand the <u>Sefer Torah</u> to the Bar/Bat Mitzvah, have an <u>aliyah</u> and recite the <u>Shehecheyanu</u> together.

What forms of participation in Jewish ritual are appropriate and inappropriate for non-Jews? (See "Exploring Jewish Prayer and Ritual" in <u>Section Two</u>.)

How can we approach the conflict between the integrity of Jewish worship and the sanctity of the family that the example raises? What will you tell Tommy's mother and what conflicts do you feel about your response?

****

SCENARIO B

ROLE OF NON-JEWS IN GOVERNANCE OF THE SYNAGOGUE

Helen Greenberg is not Jewish but she has been an active member of Temple Shalom for 20 years. She has been very effective as the Vice-President of the Sisterhood. The president of Sisterhood has suddenly resigned, which means that Helen would assume the presidency. At Temple Shalom the presidents of affiliates sit on the Board. This congregation also has a policy that non-Jews may not sit on the Board. What should be done?

****

SCENARIO C

DEALING WITH CHILDREN WHO ARE UNCLEAR ABOUT THEIR RELIGIOUS IDENTITY

You are talking with the third grade class about Chanukah. One of the students raises her hand and says, "My mom and I have been talking about Christmas. Why don't we learn about Jesus in religious school?" You know that the child's mother is not practicing her religion but has not converted to Judaism. How do you respond to the child?

How can we help our religious school teachers to respond sensitively to the questions raised by the children in their classrooms who have non-Jewish relatives?

How can we help the children of intermarried couples develop a positive Jewish identity?

How can we teach that Jews and Christians are different without diminishing the inherent validity of either Judaism or Christianity?

How can we encourage the child of an intermarried family to talk about all parts of his or her family without feeling uncomfortable?

How can the religious school offer support to those intermarried couples who are raising their children as Jews?

What kinds of programs could your Temple sponsor to help Jews-by-Choice, intermarried couples and Jews-by-Birth discuss the dilemma they all face during Chanukah and Christmas?

Note: For guidance in this area, see:
To See the World Through Jewish Eyes - Guidelines for Outreach Education: Developing Sensitivity to the Needs of Children Who Have Non-Jewish Relatives (UAHC, 1986)

EXERCISE VI

THE JEWISH SURVIVAL GAME

Objectives:

1. To enhance positive Jewish identity
2. To explore our personal commitments to Judaism
3. To explore how we can help ensure Jewish survival

Time Required:

One to one and one-half hours

Materials Needed:

A packet of the twenty 3X5 survival cards for each participant

Instructions for the Facilitator:

Arrange chairs in groups of ten, either around a table, or without a table. The table makes it somewhat easier to work since there are 3X5 cards to shuffle and rearrange. Ask the group to sit with people they do not know well, if possible. A recorder is selected by each group to keep notes on discussion and to report back to the large group. Each person is given a set of 3X5 cards. The top card should read "The Jewish Survival Game." The remaining 20 cards should each have concepts, terms, values and concerns which relate to Judaism and the Jewish people written on it. The order is not important.

Suggestions for the 20 cards include:

Jewish education	Tzedakah
Jews marrying only other Jews	State of Israel
Larger Jewish families	Kashrut
Judaism as a religion	God/Covenant
Jewish communal service organizations	Torah - Jewish law
Anti-Semitism	Jewish family
Judaism as a peoplehood	Hebrew
Shabbat	Ritual
Ethical living	Synagogue
Every Jew must help all other Jews	Prayer

The game involves choosing priorities and achieving group consensus. The leader explains that each person has been given a set of cards. Participants will be given three major tasks, one by one. The <u>first task</u> is to eliminate 3 cards from these 20. Suppose, for example, you had to form a new Jewish community. If you were <u>forced</u> to, which three would you eliminate? Each individual should first make this selection by him or herself. Then, the group of ten must come to a consensus about which three to eliminate within a given period of time (about 10 minutes).

The leader explains that the reason "anti-Semitism" is included is that many Jews hold to the philosophy that without a negative force in Jewish community life, we may not survive. According to this view, anti-Semitism provides a common threat which binds us together. In this limited sense, it can be seen as a factor in Jewish survival.

The second task is then given. Eliminate three more cards. The same procedure is followed. Again, allow about 10 minutes.

Sometime early in the program the leader should explain that this is a theoretical, hypothetical situation. It does not mean that we intend in actuality to eliminate any of these things from Jewish life. Let us look at this exercise for educational purposes and not assume that we are in fact eliminating anything from Judaism. The fact that we are eliminating three or six things from the pile of cards does not mean that they are unimportant, but rather that they are to some slight degree less important than the others. This will help some reluctant literalists to get into the fun of the discussion.

When tasks one and two are completed, assign the third task. This involves selecting the three highest priority cards from among the 14 remaining ones. This task is accomplished as before: each individual selects his or her three top priority cards, then the small groups reach consensus. (10 minutes)

When the time is expired, the leader asks the group recorder from each group to report on that group's consensus for each of the three tasks. Which three cards were eliminated each time, and why? Which three were selected as being the highest priority, and why? Allow a total of about 30 minutes for these reports.

Because different groups often take different lengths of time to achieve consensus, it is important not to wait for any one group to finish if it seems to be taking a longer time than the rest of the groups. A group that has selected only one or two can move on to the next task. Also, if there is an irreconcilable difference, the recorder may give a majority and minority report.

At any point during the reports, other members of a small group can add to the report of the spokesperson if that person feels that something has been omitted. The leader should conduct the proceedings with flexibility, and move the action along at a swift pace to keep the program and discussion lively and productive.

Close with discussion on how these concepts, terms, values and concerns which relate to Judaism and the Jewish people are transmitted and by whom. What do we mean by "Jewish survival?"

Are non-Jews capable of understanding Jewish concerns and values? Are they able to transmit these values and concerns to their Jewish children? How can the congregation assist and support non-Jews who have chosen to raise their children as Jews? How can we help our congregants understand that it is possible for non-Jews to be committed to Jewish survival?

SECTION TWO

GUIDANCE FROM OUR TRADITION

Carefully considered decisions about Reform Jewish practice can be made only after studying traditional texts and weighing current circumstances in light of the wisdom of past generations. The following three exercises provide background material for such study and set parameters for discussion of the complex issues surrounding the role of non-Jews in the synagogue.

I. EXPLORING JEWISH PRAYER AND RITUAL

Objectives:

1. To familiarize synagogue leadership with some relevant categories of Jewish ritual

2. To provide a basis for deciding whether leadership roles in ritual can appropriately be given to non-Jews

3. To familiarize non-Jewish potential participants in synagogue rituals with some basic Jewish prayer and ritual concepts

Time Required:

Ninety minutes to two hours

Materials Needed:

Comfortable room large enough for all participants to sit in a circle, around a table, or in some configuration which allows them to interact; handouts for each participant containing the brief descriptions of each category; questionnaires for each participant; pads and pencils for everyone

Instructions for the Facilitator:

This resource is appropriate to be used for either of two groups (though probably not both groups together): a synagogue ritual committee, Board of Trustees, or other body constituted to decide policy regarding non-Jews' participation in public ritual or a group of intermarried couples who are members of the congregation.

In either case Resource 1 is distributed. The facilitator informs the group that the resource contains brief expositions of a variety of terms, liturgical formulations, and non-verbal ritual actions basic to Jewish public worship. The group might read the items aloud, stopping whenever anyone requires clarification. A general discussion follows.

Alternatively, the facilitator divides the group into pairs or triads. Each subgroup finds a corner, reads the text aloud, and discusses the issues that arise. One partner would act as a reporter, summarizing his/her subgroup's comments to the whole group when it reconvenes.

<u>A program for non-Jews and their Jewish spouses concludes here with a wrap-up. A program for temple leadership continues with the following exercise</u>.

The leader distributes Resource 2, "Questionnaire for Those Who Determine Synagogue Ritual Policy." Participants respond to the questions individually or, at the discretion of the leader, in tandem with others in newly formed subgroups.

To provide closure, the leader brings participants together, ascertains the results of the questionnaire (possibly by using a blackboard tally), and allows participants to express their personal views of the results. The leader ends by asking: "Do you think that your position has changed even slightly since the beginning of this session? If so, how and why?"

(Prepared by Rabbi Lester Bronstein)

Resource 1

Jewish Communal Ritual:
Some Terms, Formulas, and Concepts

Section One: Liturgical Texts

This section examines verbal formulas which occur frequently in Jewish public ritual. The leader to recites these him/herself, or leads the assembly in such recitation.

Category A: Formulas wherein the reciter identifies personally with the Jewish people, with Jewish history, or with the Covenant of Judaism:

1) בָּרוּךְ אַתָּה, יְיָ אֱלֹהֵינוּ, מֶלֶךְ הָעוֹלָם, אֲשֶׁר קִדְּשָׁנוּ בְּמִצְוֹתָיו וְצִוָּנוּ...

Baruch atah adonai eloheynu melech haolam, asher kidshanu b'mitzvotav v'tzivanu...("Blessed are You, O Eternal our God, Sovereign of the universe, who has made us holy by Your commandments and commanded us to...")

This is the rabbinic formulation for the beracha (blessing). It accompanies all sacred acts which biblical or rabbinic dictum requires Jews to perform at prescribed times. Examples of such acts are: lighting Sabbath and festival candles, eating ritual foods like matzah and horseradish at the Passover seder, circumcising an eight-day-old boy, reciting the Shema in the morning or evening, or engaging in the study of sacred texts. The reciters are literally stating that they believe themselves to be commanded by God to perform these acts as part of a general process of sanctification ("who has made us holy by Your commandments"). With few exceptions, these are rituals unique to the practice of Judaism, and are not universalistic ethical injunctions.

2) ...אֲשֶׁר בָּחַר-בָּנוּ מִכָּל-הָעַמִּים

...asher bachar banu mikol ha-amin ("...Who has chosen us from among all peoples")

This is another rabbinic formulation derived from various biblical passages where God makes a specific covenant with one of the forebears of Israel (as, for example, with Abraham in Genesis 12). This particular version is found in the blessing preceding the public reading of the Torah ("You have chosen us from among all peoples and given us Your Torah"). Reciters of this phrase identify themselves with the people of Israel, recalling that they have been divinely chosen for certain earthly tasks. There is no explicit indication here that other peoples might not also have been divinely called for specific purposes. Nor is this a statement of Jewish superiority. The reciters merely indicate that they acknowledge their particular obligations as Jews. The Sabbath <u>Kiddush</u> expresses this same idea in the phrase "For you have chosen us and distinguished us (in a sacred way) from all peoples." Some humanistically inclined Jews recite these passages as a positive acknowledgement of their Jewishness, rather than as a belief that God would (or could) somehow single out any one people. Other Jews object to the tone of these phrases and substitute altogether different formulas.

3) ‏...וְלֹא שָׂמָנוּ כְּמִשְׁפְּחוֹת הָאֲדָמָה

...v'lo samanu k'mishp'chot ha-adamah ("Who has not made us like the other nations, and Who has not situated us like the other families of the earth")

This is a segment of a larger public statement of faith known as the <u>Aleinu</u> ("It is incumbent upon us to praise the God of all"). The formulation appears in the earliest Jewish prayerbooks from the ninth century onward and is found at the end of every Jewish worship service. It juxtaposes the universal (the "God of all", the "Maker of Creation") with the particular ("Who has not made us like the other nations"). Reciters of this formula thus summarize their belief that the universal God who governs all peoples, in fact all creation, nonetheless expects certain behaviors from Jews in particular because of the Covenant that God made with the Jewish people. As with formula #2 above, some Jews either reinterpret this paragraph humanistically or substitute other versions.

4) ‏שְׁמַע יִשְׂרָאֵל: יְיָ אֱלֹהֵינוּ, יְיָ אֶחָד

Shema yisrael, adonai eloheynu, adonai echad ("Hear, O Israel, the Eternal is our God, the Eternal is One")

This is a biblical quotation (Deuteronomy 6:4) which became a central creed and is recited at both morning and evening services. There is strong evidence that it held a key position in the liturgy of the ancient Temple long before our present forms of Jewish worship were developed. In its biblical context it is presented as a form of public liturgical declaration, reaffirming the covenant of Torah for a people who would soon experience the national and spiritual crisis of their leader Moses' death. It is phrased as a charge <u>to</u> the Jewish people. As such, it could be recited by anyone. But it quickly switches to the first person plural, "<u>our</u> God," indicating that whoever recites the <u>Shema</u> identifies him/herself with the people being addressed.

Category B: The following are examples of formulas wherein the reciter acknowledges or seeks God's particular favor for the Jewish people. (The reciter does not necessarily identify him/herself personally as a Jew.)

1) בָּרוּךְ אַתָּה, יְיָ, אוֹהֵב עַמּוֹ יִשְׂרָאֵל

Baruch atah adonai ohev amo yisrael ("Blessed are You, O Eternal; You love Your people Israel")

Recited in the evening service immediately prior to the Shema, this is an ancient rabbinic formulation, similar in theme to #2 and #3 above. Like #1 above it is a beracha (blessing), though in this form its reciter makes no mention of being "sanctified" or "commanded" to do or say something.

2) בָּרוּךְ אַתָּה, יְיָ, הַבּוֹחֵר בְּעַמּוֹ יִשְׂרָאֵל בְּאַהֲבָה

Baruch atah adonai habocher b'amo yisrael b'ahavah ("Blessed are You, O Eternal; in love You choose Your people Israel")

This is the morning version of the blessing discussed in the preceding entry. Statements made there apply here.

3) צוּר יִשְׂרָאֵל, קוּמָה בְּעֶזְרַת יִשְׂרָאֵל

Tzur yisrael, kuma b'ezrat yisrael... ("O Rock of Israel, arise to Israel's aid...")

This paragraph from the morning service invokes God's active intercession on behalf of the Jewish people. It immediately follows a liturgical retelling of Israel's exodus from Egyptian slavery.

4) הוּא יַעֲשֶׂה שָׁלוֹם עָלֵינוּ וְעַל כָּל־יִשְׂרָאֵל

Hu ya'aseh shalom aleynu v'al kol yisrael ("May God establish peace for us and for all Israel")

Recited in every Jewish service at the end of the Kaddish, it asks God for the blessing of peace for Israel. Since grammatically, it is not clear who the "us" is, the reciter coould construe the statement as one which avoids direct identification with Jews and Judaism.

Section Two: Extra-Textual Elements

The previous section dealt with the inherent meaning of the liturgical text. This section deals with the extra-textual dimension of the worship service, which provides the context for the textual and which in itself carries meaning. For instance, the "choreography" of the service, who stands where and who says what, communicates a message.

In addition, kavod ha-tzibur also informs congregational expectations of the worship experience. Kavod ha-tzibur (the honor of the congregation) is the Jewish concept that relates to a sensitivity to the time-honored values of a congregation and certain expectations which participants have of their Jewiush religious environment. For instance, there is an assumption in all congregations that persons who identify themselves as rabbis and cantors have had a prescribed period of training and education; if that is found not to be true, it violates expectations. n the same way, those who have grown up as Jews have the expectation that those who lead the congregation in prayer or who bless the Torah are Jews. When one who is not a Jew performs those specific acts, it can prove unsettling to a congregation assembled in worship. (This is not only true of Judaism. For example, Catholics would be unsettled if a non-Catholic went forward to take communion.)

1) **Lifting, rolling, dressing, carrying, blessing, or reading from the Torah scroll**

These rituals have their earliest roots in the late sixth century B.C.E. when Jews returned from Babylonian captivity and began reading the Torah regularly in public. While the specifics developed over the centuries, their collective purpose is to display the Torah before the public as a powerful symbol of the divine covenant with Israel. Generally, one person blesses the Torah and then another reads from the Torah. The one who blesses is considered to have fulfilled the mitzvah of reading from the Torah. Hagbah, the custom of lifting an open Torah scroll in order to hold the Torah script up to the view of the entire congregation, goes back at least to the seventh century C.E. Lifting, rolling, dressing and carrying the Torah are viewed as honors which are bestowed upon individuals who are participating in the worship service. The entire congregation recites a verbal formula while these ritual acts are performed.

2) **Publicly blessing the Sabbath or festival candles**

Traditionally, this mitzvah (commandment) has been a private, home-based ritual. But today, in many synagogues, this private ritual has been added to the communal service.

3) **Leading the communal worship service (in whole or in part)**

Adult male Jews are required by Jewish law to recite prescribed services three times each day. Reform Judaism teaches that men and women share equally in the responsibility to fulfill the <u>mitzvah</u> of prayer. Private recitation is totally acceptable, though public worship is deemed preferable. If one worships publicly, one is allowed to appoint a designated leader, known as a <u>sheliach tzibur</u>, (emissary of the community), to recite certain key elements of the service. By praying along with the leader, <u>or</u> by uttering an assenting "amen" to the leader's recitations, one may fulfill one's worship requirement. A leader cannot technically fulfill another's obligation unless the leader is personally obligated to recite the service to the same extent as the worshippers are. Thus the leader must consider him/herself personally commanded to perform the task of worship.

* * *

Resource 2

Questionnaire for Those Who Determine Synagogue Ritual Policy

1) Do you perceive a qualitative difference between a <u>verbal</u> and <u>non-verbal</u> involvement in a public ritual?

2) If you answered "yes" to #1: Which of the two is the more important from the worshippers' point of view? Why?

3) If you answered "no" to #1: Explain why you feel that both types of involvement might have equal impact on the worshippers?

4) Would you tend to be more lenient about a non-Jew's leading one type of ritual rather than the other? About a non-Jew's reciting one type of formula rather than another? Explain.

5) Do you take the term <u>sheliach tzibur</u> (emissary of the community, i.e. the worship leader) to be more literal or more symbolic? Explain.

6) How does your answer to #5 influence your decision to allow/disallow a non-Jew to serve as the <u>sheliach tzibur</u> and to conduct public ritual?

7) Do you take such phrases as "Who made us holy by Your commandments and commanded us..." and "You chose us from among all peoples" to be more literal or more symbolic? Explain.

8) Does performing an extra-textual ritual constitute an act of <u>shlichut tzibur</u> (being an emissary of the congregation)? Explain.

9) Are all forms of public extra-textual involvement viewed in the same way, i.e. is sitting on the <u>bimah</u> or opening the ark doors viewed in the same way as lifting, dressing or carrying the Torah?

10) If a particular act or recitation by a non-Jew were technically not a violation of Jewish tradition, would you thereby support it? Or would you oppose it if you felt that nonetheless such involvement goes against the <u>spirit</u> of Jewish tradition?

11) What public acts or recitations would you want to allow a non-Jew to perform in your synagogue? What criteria would you ultimately use?

II. THE ROLE OF THE NON-JEW IN THE SYNAGOGUE: SETTING THE DISCUSSION IN CONTEXT

Objective:

To examine how our tradition has grappled with the role of non-Jews within the Jewish community during various times and in different contexts

Target Audience:

Congregational leadership and/or adult discussion groups

Time Required:

One hour

Material Needed:

A copy of the text for each participant

Instructions for the Facilitator:

When considering the role of the non-Jew in the synagogue for both membership and ritual purposes, it is helpful to begin with a discussion of the longevity and intractibility of this issue. By anchoring the dilemma to its historical context, it becomes readily apparent to those struggling with the issue that:

1) they are engaged in discussion of an issue that has been of concern for millenia

2) they are not dealing with the issue in isolation; it has received both historical and contemporary attention. This discussion is designed to help defuse the heavy artillery that tends to be brought out on both sides of the issue and lends a measure of validation to each perspective

While our tradition has grappled with the role of non-Jews within the Jewish community during various times and in different contexts, Torah does not contain one answer, but describes two opposite poles. Each congregation must find its own level of comfort.

Begin by providing participants with copies of the following passages from Ezra and Ruth. Provide the context of each passage before asking a volunteer to read each one to the group.

Ask participants for their reactions to each passage and discuss. The following points should be made by the facilitator:

EZRA Passage:

1. This passage reflects an <u>institutional</u> response, aimed at saving the Jewish people.

2. Note the similarities to contemporary synagogue organization: there is a leader, an advisor, an executive committee. There are lists, meetings, postponements and, finally, a policy that is presented as "sealed, stamped, and delivered." There are many parallels with temple politics.

3. Note that there is no personal focus on the individuals affected by the policy.

4. The action taken was seen as necessary for the survival of the Jewish people.

RUTH Passage:

1. This passage reflects a <u>non-institutional</u> response which, in effect, saves the Jewish people as well. (Ruth is the great-grandmother of King David from whose line the Messiah will come).

2. Ruth was intermarried (with Naomi's son); she becomes the prototype of the <u>ger tzedek</u>.

3. Imagine how Naomi must have treated Ruth so that Ruth <u>begged</u> to go with her.

4. Outreach in the contemporary Reform community is an effort to <u>institutionalize</u> this kind of <u>personal</u> response.

To conclude the discussion, note that the Bible presents both sides of the issue, but does not offer a prescribed middle ground. The synagogue is a uniquely Jewish <u>institution</u>. Our challenge is to balance institutional needs with a personal welcoming response. The task at hand is to negotiate a policy for yourselves. It will not be easy, but you will follow in a good tradition.

(Prepared by Dru Greenwood)

Ezra 10:1-4;9-11

(1) While Ezra was praying and making confession, weeping and prostrating himself before the House of God, a very great crowd of Israelites gathered about him, men, women, and children; the people were weeping bitterly. (2) Then Shecaniah son of Jehiel of the family of Elam spoke up and said to Ezra, "We have trespassed against our God by bringing into our homes foreign women from the peoples of the land; but there is still hope for Israel despite this. (3) Now then, let us make a covenant with our God to expel all these women and those who have been born to them, in accordance with the bidding of the Lord and of all who are concerned over the commandment of our God, and let the teaching be obeyed. (4) Take action, for the responsibility is yours and we are with you. Act with resolve!"

(9) All the men of Judah and Benjamin assembled in Jerusalem in three days; it was the ninth month, the twentieth of the month. All the people sat in the square of the House of God, trembling on account of the event and because of the rains. (10) Then Ezra the priest got up and said to them, "You have trespassed by bringing home foreign women, thus aggravating the guilt of Israel. (11) So now, make confession to the Lord, God of your fathers, and do His will, and separate yourselves from the peoples of the land and from the foreign women."

*   *   *

Ruth 1:14-19

(14) They broke into weeping again, and Orpah kissed her mother-in-law farewell. But Ruth clung to her. (15) So she said, "See, your sister-in-law has returned to her people and her gods. Go follow your sister-in-law." (16) But Ruth replied, "Do not urge me to leave you, to turn back and not follow you. For I will go; wherever you lodge, I will lodge; your people shall be my people, and your God my God. (17) Where you die, I will die, and there I will be buried. Thus and more may the Lord do to me if anything but death parts me from you." (18) When [Naomi] saw how determined she was to go with her; she ceased to argue with her, (19) and the two went on until they reached Bethlehem.

III. GUIDANCE FROM OUR SOURCES: REFORM JEWISH RESPONSA

May a non-Jew bless Shabbat candles? Is gambling for synagogue fundraising permissable? Can a toupé serve as a yarmulka? These are among the thousands of questions that have been submitted to rabbinical authorities in the past and present. They and their answers, the responsa, have become part of the Halakhah, the legal thought of Judaism.

In every generation Jews confront new situations which require contemporary solutions. Questions (she'elot) and answers (teshuvot) covering every aspect of Jewish life are exchanged between the inquirers and the rabbis. Key responsa are then collected and arranged into volumes of case law for determining future decisions. In addition to their value as legal precedents, these compendia provide scholars with a wealth of historic information about the daily lives and communal issues of Jews from medieval North Africa to present-day North America. Drawing on traditional texts, the Reform movement has evolved its own responsa literature.

Reform Judaism has always prided itself on providing a religious framework that was responsive to the issues of the day, yet it has consistently used Jewish history and its sages for guidance. From a Reform perspective, Jewish sources provide perspective and guidance, rather than ultimate authority. The issue of the role of the non-Jew in the synagogue has sent us back to our sources for food-for-thought, guidance, and inspiration.

How does Reform responsa evolve? While the issues may be enormously complex, the process is rather simple:

HOW THE REFORM RESPONSA COMMITTEE WORKS

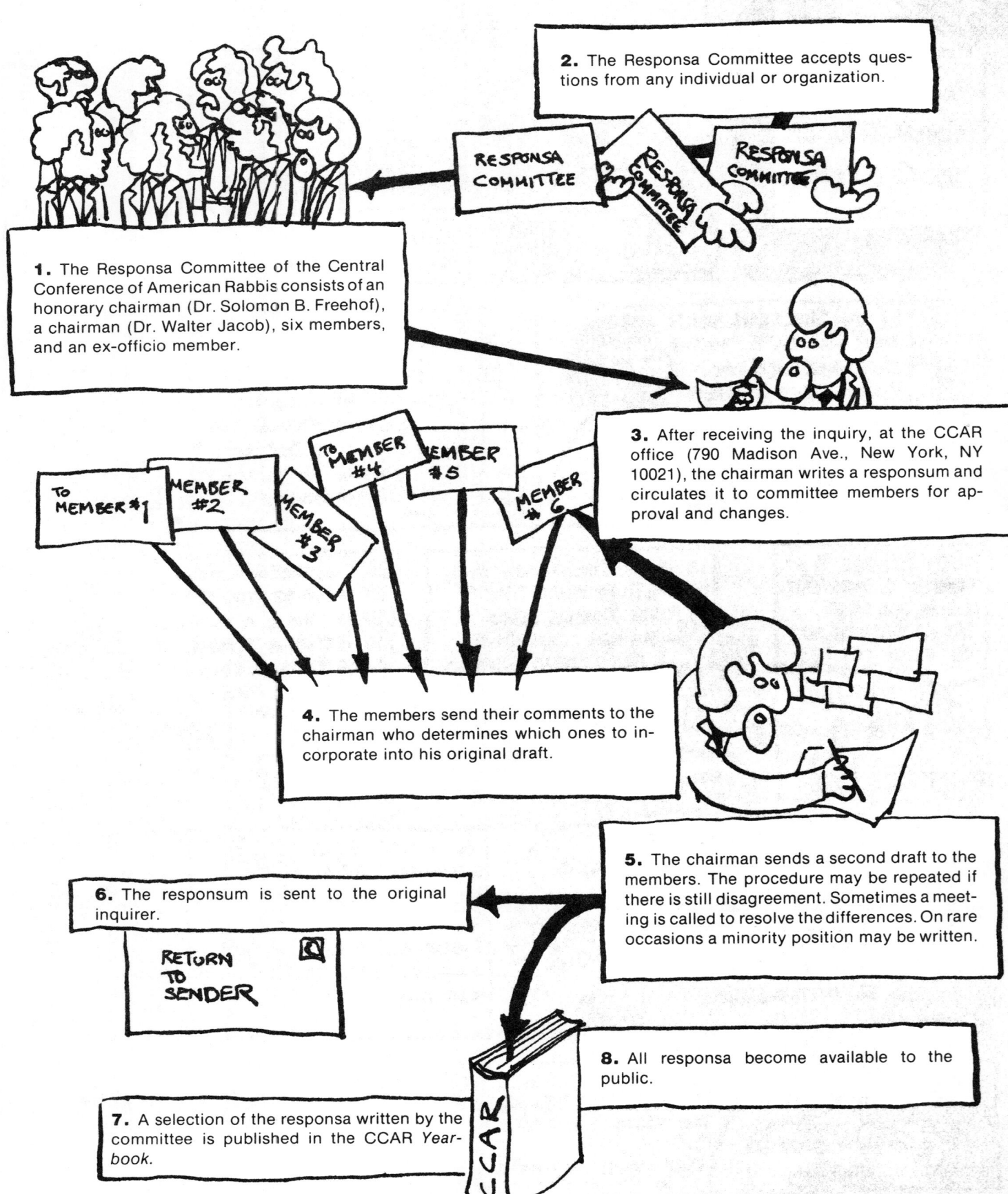

In Section Three of this packet, Rabbi Sally Priesand's article, "The Role of the Non-Jew and the Temple Constitution," describes how her congregation turned to Jewish sources for guidance in their decision making. In this chapter you will find a selection of Reform responsa related to the role of the non-Jew in the synagogue. The questions asked range from "Can a Gentile join a congregation?" to "To what extent may non-Jews participate in a Jewish public service?" The answers will provide you with a deepened appreciation of the vitality of Jewish sources, and the irrevocable bond between past and present in our tradition.

---

*   This discussion is based on material from <u>Keeping Posted</u>, Vol. XXIV, No. 6, March 1979, UAHC. The illustrations are reprinted with permission from <u>Keeping Posted</u> and were created by Joel Grishaver, Creative Chair of Tora Aura Productions.

*   The current address of the CCAR is 192 Lexington Avenue, New York, NY 10016.

SELECTED REFORM RESPONSA

161. GENTILES IN A JEWISH CONGREGATION

QUESTION: Can a Gentile who has lived a basically Jewish life, and is married to a Jewess, join a congregation in his own right? (Rabbi J. Edelstein, Monroeville, PA)

ANSWER: This Gentile would be considered a ger toshav, or a follower of the Noahide laws, but of course, we could not consider him to be a ger tsedek, or a convert to Judaism. Christians and Muslims, as monotheists, have been classified as gerei toshav since the Middles Ages (Meir of Rothenberg Responsa #386; Yad Hil. M'lakhim 8.11, Shulhan Arukh Yoreh Deah 148.2, etc.) rather than idolators. The status of a ger toshav is rather clear. A ger toshav is considered equal to a Jew in all legal matters, but he has no status in connection with ritual obligations, for they are not incumbent upon him. He would, therefore, not be considered part of the quota for a minyan or for m'zuman, nor could he lead a worship service, etc. (Shulhan Arukh Orah Hayim 199.4).

We can not include such an individual in our synagogue membership. This would, after all, entail their participation in every aspect of synagogue life, the right to lead services, the right to help determine policy on synagogue members. It would be inappropriate to have unconverted Gentiles participate in these aspects of congregational life. If this individual feels close to the congregation and wishes to help it, then he should feel free to contribute to it, attend its services and functions; perhaps later that individual will convert and join the congregation.

July 1977

Contemporary American Reform Responsa, Walter Jacob, CCAR:1987.

162. CONGREGATIONAL MEMBERSHIP FOR A NON-JEWISH SPOUSE

QUESTION: Should we reinstitute the ancient category of semi-proselyte known in the Talmudic literature as <u>yirei adonai</u>, <u>ger toshav</u> and <u>ger shaar</u>? Would this be a way of solving the problem of non-Jewish spouse whose Jewish husband or wife belong to our congregations while they, as non-Jews with a considerable interest in Judaism, have either no status or a status which has not been properly and clearly defined? Would this ancient Talmudic category help us with our modern problems? What kind of status should be granted to such an individual? (Rabbi G. Raiskin, Burlingame, CA)

ANSWER: The problem of the non-Jewish spouse is a serious one in many congregations. Every effort toward a solution deserves our attention and consideration. We should begin by looking at the Talmudic categories, <u>yirei adonai</u>, <u>gerei toshav</u> and <u>gerei shaar</u>, and try to understand their precise meaning. What rights, if any, did individuals in each category possess? How were they treated in the Temple, in the synagogue, by Jewish courts, etc?

The general question of conversion to Judaism has been well treated by a number of our colleagues (J. Rosenbloom, <u>Conversion to Judaism</u>, Cincinnati, 1978; H. Eichorn, <u>Conversion to Judaism</u>, New York, 1965; B. Bamberger, <u>Proselytism in the Talmudic Period</u>, New York, 1939; W. Braude, <u>Jewish Proselytizing in the First Five Centuries of the Common Era</u>, Providence, 1940). These volumes indicate that conversion to Judaism has continued through the centuries. They discuss what was expected of the convert, motives which led to conversion, and the way in which converts have fit into the general community. Relatively little space in these volumes is given to our categories, which existed for only a few centuries. These categories play no role in rabbinic literature after the <u>Talmud</u>, and when these terms are used they are synonymous with <u>benei noah</u>, in other words, a Gentile who had accepted basic human morality and was no longer a pagan. The terms also designate individuals who had adopted certain Jewish thoughts in the post Talmudic period. No special status has been accorded to them (S. Zeitlin, "Proselyte and Proselytism," <u>Harry Wolfson Jubilee Volumes</u>, Vol. 2, pp. 587 ff; see also A. Bertholet, <u>Die Stellung der Israeliten und der Juden zu den Fremden</u>, Leipzig, 1896). If we follow the generally accepted view, individuals characterized by these designations seem to have fallen into four categories during the Mishnaic and early Talmudic period:

1. A theoretical designation which indicated how the rabbis would have liked to treat resident aliens (<u>gerei toshav</u>) in Israel (<u>M</u>. Gerim 3.1; A. Z. 64b; San 56a ff; Arak. 29a).

2. Individuals who were on their way to becoming full proselytes but had not yet fulfilled all the conditions. In other words, they may have undergone immersion or circumcision, but not yet brought the mandatory sacrifice in Jerusalem before the destruction of the temple (Moore,

<blockquote>

Judaism in the First Centuries of the Christian Era, Vol. I, pp. 330 ff; *Mishnat R. Eliezer*, p. 374; Juvenal, *Satires*, XIV, 96ff).

3. Individuals who were married to Jews, accepted basic Jewish morality and religious thought, but for a variety of reasons were unwilling to undergo complete conversion. Usually this category seemed to consist of husbands of women who had become Jewish and were unwilling to follow as this entailed the difficult operation of circumcision. Other reasons to follow may also have been operative.

4. Individuals who had accepted some of the ethics and morality of Judaism and left their ancient pagan beliefs, in other words, a synonym for *benei noah* (A.Z. 64a; Pes. 21a; Ker. 8b; Hul. 5a; Meg. 13a; Philo, *Contra Apion*; Josephus, *Antiq.* 20.8.7; *Wars* 2.18.2, 7.3.3).

</blockquote>

One scholar, Solomon Zeitlin, felt that these categories did not exist at all. The terms merely designated Gentiles who were no longer idolaters but in no way semi-proselytes (Zeitlin, *op. cit.*).

For the purposes of our discussion, we can forget the first two categories. As we turn to the remaining category, we must first ask about the status of these individuals within the Jewish community. It is clear from a wide variety of statements that they were considered on a level above pagans, but did not possess the status of full converts or Jews; they had no official status in either the synagogue or a Jewish court and were considered non-Jews in virtually all legal matters (*Gerei Toshav*, *Encyclopedia Talmudit*, Vol. 6, pp. 290ff). They could bring sacrifices to the Temple, but so could any pagan who wished to do so (Schurer, *A History of the Jewish People in the Age of Jesus Christ*, revised by Vermez, Millar and Black, Vol. 2, pp. 309ff). The fact that they had taken this step was recognized and praised; there was the hope that they might go further, but until this occurred, no real change of status was conferred.

These designations ceased to exist with the end of the pagan period. After the majority of the neighboring people had become Christians, or later, followers of Islam, most individuals known to Jews were *benei noah* and could be designated by the synonyms, *yirei adonai*, *ger toshav*, and *ger shaar*. The special categories, therefore, became meaningless.

If we nowadays accorded these designations to our Christian friends, they would provide no special status in the synagogue but simply recognize the ethical and moral teachings of their religion as akin to our own which we have done anyhow.

A revival, therefore, of the Talmudic categories of *yirei adonai*, *ger toshav*, and *ger shaar* would not achieve the goal desired or solve the problem of the non-Jewish spouse. It is not likely that a revival of a special designation which carries no appropriate historical overtones would help us. It would probably only confuse matters and place the non-Jewish partner in a doubtful position. We, therefore, recommend that the membership section of the constitution and the constitutions of the auxiliary bodies, such as Brotherhood and Sisterhood, read as follows:

Membership in our congregation is limited to Jews and Jewish families. A non-Jewish partner is welcome to the fellowship of the congregation and is encouraged to participate in all of its activities; however, the non-Jewish spouse may not serve on the Board, hold office, become chairman of any committee or have the privilege of voting at congregational or committee meetings.

October 1983

Contemporary American Reform Responsa, Walter Jacob, CCAR:1987.

163. GENTILE CHAIRMAN OF CONFIRMATION GROUP

QUESTION: The parents of each year's Confirmation Class and of Bar/Bar Mitzvah groups form a club which sponsors special activities for these young people; it also provides some educational programs for the parents. This year a mother who is not Jewish has been selected as chairman of the Confirmation Club. This was done inadvertently as the woman in question has identified herself closely with the Jewish community and has been very active in communal work and the Jewish Federation. She attends synagogue services regularly. Although the rabbi knew that she was not Jewish, members of the group were unaware of that fact. How should we deal with this situation? (D.L., Los Angeles, CA).

ANSWER: This Committee has decided on a number of other occasions that it is inappropriate for a non-Jew to serve in leadership positions within a congregation (see "Congregational Membership for A Non-Jewish Partner"). There is, of course, nothing which would prohibit such individuals from being active in the congregation and the Jewish community. In fact, we should encourage such activities even if full conversion to Judaism is not possible. Such efforts will eventually bring these fine individuals closer to Judaism and may lead to eventual conversion.

In the case of this individual, it would be appropriate to suggest that this might be a good time to accept Judaism formally. Her activities have taken place entirely within the orbit of Judaism; her youngest child is now to be confirmed. Her own commitment and her efforts through the years would more than suffice to qualify for her conversion without any further instruction. It has been my experience that individuals in this position are very open to such a suggestion and will often formally join the community. That would, of course, remove the problem.

April 1983

Contemporary American Reform Responsa, Walter Jacob, CCAR:1987.

164. GENTILE MEMBERS ON CONGREGATIONAL COMMITTEES

QUESTION: My congregation contains a number of couples in which one spouse is Christian and the other is Jewish. Several of these non-Jews have indicated interest in working on the committees of the congregation. What limits to participation, if any, should be set? (K. S. Cleveland, OH)

ANSWER: We Jews have considered Christians as benei noah since the early Middle Ages, so all the statements made during previous periods which deal with idolatry do not apply to Christians or Moslems. Christians are monotheists who have added elements (shituf) to One God. We should note that even in the Talmudic period, there was considerable doubt about classifying pagans in the same category as the idolators of previous periods for it was clear to many of the Talmudic authorities that the old idolatrous religions had lost their hold on the people (Hul. 13b; Yad Hil. Melakhim 11; Maimonides, Moreh Nivukhim 1.71; Responsa II, #448, ed. Blau).

This age old change in our attitude and the new mood brought by the French Revolution have led to a completely different approach to the non-Jewish world. This began with the Paris Sanhedrin of 1807, which dealt with numerous questions concerning the relationship between Jews and non-Jews (Tama, Transaction of the Parisian Sanhedrin, tr. F. Kirwan; W.G. Plaut, The Rise of Reform Judaism).

The Responsa Committee, in recent years, has addressed the question of non-Jewish participation in congregational life a number of times. We have discussed their participation in religious services and life cycle events as well as burial in our cemeteries (W. Jacob, American Reform Responsa, #6, #10, #98, etc.). The Committee has stated that non-Jews should not become formal members of a congregation in a responsum (see "Non-Jews as Congregational Members"). Our congregations are established to continue and further the traditions and goals of Judaism; they are not general charities or social clubs open to everyone. In this way they differ from Hadassah, ORT, Brandeis and other groups whose constituency may be largely Jewish but has always included non-Jewish members. Many other examples could be given.

When a mixed couple joins a congregation, the membership and the voting rights should be limited to the Jewish spouse. That, of course, does not exclude the non-Jew from participation at services, educational or social functions, but means that due to the nature of the synagogue, such individuals can have no voice in its governance. This would also apply to congregational committees. Those committees which deal with matters which specifically involve Jewish knowledge or feelings must, by their nature, exclude non-Jewish participation. We must also exclude non-Jews from committees which are viewed as stepping-stones to congregational leadership.

It would, however, be perfectly possible to include non-Jews in committees of a more general nature (without a vote) which deal with community projects. For example, committees on scholarship, social action, community service, the handicapped, etc., could draw their membership from Jewish congregants as well as non-Jewish spouses. We should be careful, however, not to have non-Jews as chairpeople of these committees or as representatives of such committees to the general community.

In other words, non-Jews who wish to be active in some aspect of synagogue life should be encouraged in that direction both through membership on committees with a broad communal purpose as well as attendance at synagogue functions with the hope that they will eventually join us as fully committed Jews.

April 1983

<u>Contemporary American Reform Responsa</u>, Walter Jacob, CCAR:1987.

165. MAY A NON-JEW LIGHT THE SHABBAT EVE CANDLES?

QUESTION: May a non-Jew married to a Jew light the Shabbat eve candles? The question has arisen at the time when a son of such a couple is about to be Bar Mitzvah. Normally the mother of the Bar/Bat Mitzvah participates in the Shabbat eve ceremony by lighting the candles. May she do so under the circumstances?
(Rabbi E. Palnick, Little Rock, AR)

ANSWER: Tradition has little to say on this specifically as the custom of lighting the candles in the synagogue is an innovation of the Reform movement. It may have been intended as a revival of an ancient custom of lighting the Shabbat candles following the afternoon service in the synagogue (Siddur Rav Amram, ed., Jerusalem, 1979, p. 61, also Isaac Lamperonti, Pahad Yitzhaq, Hadlakhah). It came as a recent addition to the late Friday evening service created by Isaac Mayer Wise. His first congregation was not enthusiastic but did permit him to establish such a service in 1869 (W.G. Plaut, "The Sabbath in the Reform Movement," C.C.A.R. Yearbook, Vol. 75, p. 177). This service did not contain the ritual of lighting the candles in the synagogue, nor did the early editions of the Union Prayerbook. It was introduced in the newly revised edition of 1940 and has become an accepted part of our liturgy.

The lighting of Shabbat candles at the erev Shabbat service represents a synagogue version of the mitzvah of lighting Shabbat candles at home (M. Shab II, 6). This was one of the three mitzvot specifically commanded to women (Shulhan Arukh Orah Hayim 263.3), although both men and women may light the candles.

The non-Jewish spouse's participation in the Friday evening ritual at home has evolved naturally. Frequently she does light the Shabbat candles and through this indicates a wish to establish some ties with Judaism at home. Technically, of course, it is inappropriate for a Christian to recite the traditional benediction as it contains the words asher qidshanu -"who sanctified us with His commandments," which indicates an obligation imposed on Jews. We have, however, taken this act as a positve indication that the home is to be Jewish.

We can not apply the same reasoning to the non-Jewish mother's participation in the Friday evening service by reciting the traditional words on the occasion of her child's Bar/Bat Mitzvah. This is a public service and the non-Jews may not lead in essential segments of the synagogue service or sections which utilize such phrases as "who has sanctified us" ("Participation of Non-Jews in a Jewish Public Service," W. Jacob, American Reform Responsa, #6). The non-Jewish mother may light the candles and recite a modified prayer while someone else, perhaps another family member, should recite the traditional b'rakhah.

January 1984
Contemporary American Reform Responsa, Walter Jacob, CCAR:1987.

6. PARTICIPATION OF NON-JEWS IN A JEWISH PUBLIC SERVICE
(1979, Walter Jacob)

QUESTION: To what extent may non-Jews participate in a Jewish public service? (Committee on Education)

ANSWER: In order to answer this question properly, we must first inquire about the status of Christians in Jewish law. It is clear that from the Middle Ages onward, Christians and Moslems were considered as monotheists rather than pagans. The pattern for this may very well have been set by Hiyya bar Abba, who stated that Gentiles outside of the Land of Israel were not to be considered idolators, but merely as people who were following the practices of their ancestors (Chullin 13b). Maimonides (12th century) viewed Christians and Moslems akin to **Benei Noach**. In that capacity, they were assisting the preparation for the messianic era (**Yad**, Hil. Melachim II, **Moreh Nevuchim** I.71; **Responsa**, II no. 448 (ed. Blau). A French contemporary of Maimonides, commenting on Talmud Bechorot 2b, expressed the same feeling about Christians. All placed Christians in these special categories. We should, of course, remember that good treatment and many privileges were extended to pagans in earlier times, both in Israel and in Babylon, **mipenei darchei shalom**. We comforted their dead, visited their sick, helped their poor, etc. (Git.59b, 61a; Tur, Choshen Mishpat 266). Proper consideration was to be extended, as they were human beings despite their pagan beliefs.

The classification of Christians as **Gerei Toshav** had theological implications and also important economic consequences; for example, wine made by a Gentile was permitted to be handled by Ashkenazic Jews. Although it could not be consumed by Jews, Jews could trade in it (**Tosafot** to San. 63b; Isserles to **Sh.A.**, Y.D. 123.1). Sephardic Jews did not follow this practice and had no pressing need to do so as they were not involved in extensive wine growing and lived among Moslems whose consumption of wine was limited (Maimonides, **Responsa**, II no. 448; **Tur**, Y.D. 124).

As we turn to worship, we must remember that non-Jews were welcome to pray in the ancient Temple and Solomon had already asked that their prayers be heard by God (I Kings 8:41ff). Sacrifices of pagans were acceptable in the Temple (Mon. 73b) and the permanent gift of an item such as a **Menora** to a synagogue was also considered as perfectly acceptable (Arachin 6b). There was nothing improper about a non-Jew handling a Torah or reading from it; it is not subject to ritual uncleanliness (Ber. 22a; **Yad**, Hil. Sefer Torah X.8; **Sh.A.**, Y.D. 282.9). Statements about Gentiles studying Torah contradict each other; so on the one hand we have the phrase that non-Jews who studied Torah deserved death (i.e., are punishable by heaven), and on the other hand, an individual who studied in this fashion is considered equal to the High Priest (B.K. 38a). In the latter section, we hear of a Roman emperor who sent students to study Torah from the rabbis. David Hoffman (**Melamed Leho-il**, Y.D. 77) stated that we should teach everything except specific commandments so that the Gentile not disrespect erring Jews.

Despite this friendly attitude of Judaism towards Christianity, all of the traditional authorities made it quite clear that major distinctions continue to exist. Maimonides felt that many Christians were actual idolators and, therefore, sought to restrict relationships with them (**Yad**, Hil. Akum X.2) and also prohibited Jews from dealing in any way in Christian wine (**Yad**, Hil. Maachalot Asurot XVII); and he and all the other medieval authorities felt that both Christianity and Islam had mixed strange concepts (**shituf**) into the absolute unity of God as expressed by Judaism (Isserles to **Shulchan Aruch**, Orach Chayim 156; Maimonides, **Pe-er Hador**, 50; etc.). In secular relationships Christians could be treated as **Benei Noach**, but in religious matters distinctions were to remain.

Now, let us deal with the specific matter of prayer recited by an idolator or a Christian. If an idolator recited a prayer, i.e., a private prayer, in the name of God, those who heard it were to respond with "**Amen**" (Ber. 44a; Isserles to **Sh.A.**, O.Ch. 215.2). The only references to Christians participating in Jewish public worship in rabbinic literature which I have been able to find consisted of singers, who honored the bride and groom by singing for them on Shabbat (H. Benvenisti, **Keneset Hagedola**, quoted in Palligi, **Lev Chayim** II.9). A similar statement has already been made by Eliezer ben Joel Halevi (**Raviah**, 796). In these cases, we are dealing with instrumental music played on the Sabbath in honor of the bride and groom by non-Jews. Citations, both for and against this practice, are listed in **Sede Chemed**, Ma-arechet Chatan Vechala, no. 13.

From Babylonian times onward, public prayers for rulers of the country, parallel to those for scholars and students in the academies, were included in the liturgy and have remained there ever since. These rulers, of course, were pagans, Moslems, or Christians. We, in modern times, have gone a number of steps further than this. For example, we regularly recite the names of non-Jewish dead in the lists of deceased read before the **Kaddish**. In most cases, these are relatives of converts; although the convert is not duty-bound to mourn for his parents, he should be encouraged to do so out of respect (**Yad**, Hil. Evel 2.3; Radbaz to **Yad**; **Sh.A.**, Y.D. 374.5; and many subsequent authorities). We have, however, also added the names of notable Christians from time to time. In addition, we have participated frequently in interfaith services, which have generally been associated with national holidays or events; these have usually been non-liturgical in character, i.e., consisted of Biblical readings and various prayers without following the strict order of the service. Furthermore, we have invited non-Jews, including ministers and priests, to address our congregations during our public services. This practice has been widespread in the Reform and Conservative movements. Thus, there is no doubt that we have included priests, ministers, and non-Jewish participants in our services in a manner not known heretofore. In addition, nowadays, because of intermarriage we find the non-Jewish parent involved in a Bar/Bat Mitzvah. It would be appropriate to have that parent participate in some way in the service, but not in the same way as a Jewish parent. For example, he or she should not recite the traditional blessing over the Torah which includes the words **"asher bachar banu."** It would be well if he/she recited a special blessing, perhaps akin to the words suggested by Solomon B. Freehof: "Praised be Thou, Lord our God, King of the Universe, Who has given His sacred law unto all His children that we may learn, observe, and serve Him in righteousness" (Current Reform Responsa, p. 91).

We have, therefore, gone much further than any generation before our time by permitting non-Jews a larger role in our public services; this is part of a more open and friendly interreligious attitude which the Reform movement has encouraged and led. Yet, these steps have remained within definite limits. We have not included non-Jews, no matter how friendly, in the essential elements of the service.

If we follow the line of reasoning which divides between the essential service and supplemental prayers and statements, we may conclude that Christians, Moslems, and other non-Jews who fall into the category of **Benei Noach** may participate in a public service in any of the following ways: (1) through anything which does not require specific statement from them, i.e., by standing and silently witnessing whatever is taking place (e.g. as a member of a wedding party or as a pallbearer); (2) through the recitation of special prayers added to the service at non-liturgical community-wide services; commemorations, and celebrations (Thanksgiving, etc.); (3) through the recitation of prayers for special family occasions (Bar/Bat Mitzvah of children raised as Jews, at a wedding or funeral, etc.). All such prayers and statements should reflect the mood of the service and be non-Christological in nature.

Walter Jacob, Chairman
Leonard S. Kravitz
Eugene Lipman
Harry A. Roth

Rav A. Soloff
Bernard Zlotowitz
W. Gunther Plaut

American Reform Responsa, Walter Jacob, Ed., CCAR: 1983.

10. SYNAGOGUE MEMBERSHIP OF A MIXED COUPLE
(Vol. XCII, 1982, pp. 215-216)

QUESTION: In these days of rising mixed marriages, should we extend Temple membership to the non-Jewish member in a mixed family? (Rabbi Prystowsky, Lafayette Hill, Pennsylvania)

ANSWER: It is clear from tradition that such marriages cannot be considered as **Kiddushin (Yad. Hil. Ishut 15; Shulchan Aruch**, Even Ha-ezer 154.23) and, of course, the CCAR has expressed its views for the Reform movement (Resolution, CCAR Yearbook, vol. 83, p. 97; Responsum, CCAR Yearbook, vol. 90 pp. 86 ff). However, we have recognized these marriages as civil marriages and are quite willing, even eager, to have the children raised as Jews. Clearly, the children of such marriages will often become Jewish, and so a major portion of the family--father or mother and children--will have a role in the religious life of the synagogue.

This need not involve full synagogue membership of the non-Jewish family partner. Most synagogues, on their application forms, require some sort of statement of identity with Judaism as the religion, and certainly such an individual could not in good conscience sign this if he/she remains a Christian. Naturally, we would expect the Jewish party to assume his/her full responsibilities for the financial maintenance of the synagogue, especially as children will be educated by the synagogue.

Full membership in the congregation would also imply the ability to become a member of the Board of Trustees and an officer of the congregation. This could very likely lead to an absurd condition in which a Jewish congregation would have a non-Jewish officer whose knowledge of the workings of the synagogue would be gained only from the practical organizational experience but without any Jewish background. Rather than risking these kinds of conditions, it would be better for the synagogue to arrange that membership be held by the Jewish partner, even in those congregations in which the membership is normally held by the entire family. This would spare the congregation and the individual embarrassment.

This has been the traditional response of Reform Judaism (Solomon B. Freehof, Recent Reform Responsa, pp. 63ff) and continues to be our view.

We would continue to encourage the non-Jewish partner to be buried in our cemetery, provided that there were no specific Christian ritual or no specific markings on the tombstone. Even if that individual chose not to become Jewish, he or she would certainly be welcome at all functions of the synagogue but would not qualify for membership.

Walter Jacob, Chairman	Isaac Neuman	Rav A. Soloff
Joseph Glaser	W. Gunther Plaut	Sheldon Zimmerman
Leonard S. Kravitz	Harry A. Roth	Bernard Zlotowitz
Simeon Maslin	Herman Schaalman	

<u>American Reform Responsa</u>, Walter Jacob, Ed., CCAR: 1983.

Selections from <u>American Reform Responsa</u> and <u>Contemporary American Reform Responsa</u> are copyright by the Central Conference of American Rabbis and used by permission.

SECTION THREE

ESSAYS

Non-Jews and Jewish Life-Cycle Liturgy

by Rabbi Lawrence A. Hoffman
Professor of Liturgy
Hebrew Union College-Jewish Institute of Religion

The Challenge

The very idea that non-Jews would want to recite Jewish liturgy should not be taken lightly. It is a sign of how far we have come in the grand experiment of pluralism that may in the long run turn out to be North America's greatest contribution to human history. That Jews or Christians would ever opt willingly even to be present, let alone to participate, at each other's ritual occasions is a phenomenon that is still less than a few decades old. Predictably, therefore, congregations wonder how responsibly to welcome it.

Not all situations of interfaith prayer are identical. First, there are cases in which <u>we worship in common</u>: a Thanksgiving Day service, for example, that takes place in a church or synagogue, with a worshipping congregation of Jews and Christians drawn from an entire community. Alternatively, we find regularly now what we can call an <u>indigenous service with guests</u>, that is, a regular Jewish worship service in which Christians are present as guests: Jews inviting non-Jewish friends to their home <u>seder</u>, for example; or to synagogue services, for a Bar/Bat Mitzvah; or (as I recently observed) college students returning home for Yom Kippur, and bringing non-Jewish roommates along for the experience. These latter instances are not worship in common, in that with the exception of some words of welcome or explanations to the guests, the service remains (religiously speaking) exactly what it would have been if the guests had not been there.[1] There is, however, yet a third category: life-cycle ceremonies which are indigenous in that they emerge from Jewish tradition, but which differ in kind from the normal indigenous service with guests, in that non-Jewish relatives of the family are cast in the ambivalent role of reciting prayers or performing actions that normally only Jews would be doing. This third category, <u>life-cycle liturgies with mixed-married families</u> is apt to be particularly unsettling for all concerned.

A typical case is a non-Jewish parent of a Bar/Bat Mitzvah. Frequently, Bar/Bat Mitzvah parents bless the Shabbat candles and/or recite <u>Kiddush</u> at Friday night services. At the Bar/Bat Mitzvah ritual the next morning, they may be expected to receive an <u>aliyah</u>, or to take part in a non-traditional but highly emotional ceremony of passing the Torah down through the generations. A non-Jewish parent will necessarily be thrust into a severe conflict on any or all of these things, as will the congregation, which tries to balance appropriate pastoral concern on one hand, and appropriate religious consciousness on the other. What guidance can we offer to congregations and mixed-married families, as they wrestle with these quandaries?

On Reading Jewish Texts
Many of us harbor the hope that Jewish sources themselves offer clear guidance, our problem being (we imagine) that we need only read enough pages of Talmud, responsa, or liturgical and ethical literature. The fact is, however, that modern literary criticism demonstrates quite convincingly that no text in the world exists independently of the reading strategy of the reader. Jewish sources do say something, naturally, but exactly how they speak to modern-day Jews intent on learning from them, and how those same Jews read the texts in question, are complex matters indeed.

Traditional responsa, for example, assume that an unqualified talmudic opinion normally takes priority over an opposing view -- or, at least, an opposing view for which there is no prior traditional sanction -- that is held by a modern authority. Similarly, they follow established rules that govern unresolved debates between known rabbis of the past, so that sources describing Rabbi X and Rabbi Y in dialogue can be reconciled by looking up where these two rabbis stand on the pecking order of authoritativeness, and following the opinion of the one who is higher up the ladder. Finally, in the case of a known majority position in the past coupled with a minority report from the same era, traditional writers of responsa are generally duty-bound to follow the majority, even though they might find the minority opinion more appealing to their ethical sensibility. Reform respondents, on the other hand, have been less willing to privilege talmudic rabbis over moderns; they rarely consult the rules of rabbinic debate; and they overturn majority rulings with minority views that reflect a modern sense of moral propriety. There are other differences also: many traditionalists see Jewish tradition as an undifferentiated whole, for example, in which the <u>context</u> of an opinion has little relevance,[2] whereas liberals view the historical context as highly significant, and differentiate texts on the basis of historical development. For the former, what was right in the third century and the 12th century and the 18th century must necessarily be right in the 20th century and the 25th century; for the latter, third-century Zoroastrian Babylonia, 12th-century Moslem Egypt, 18th-century Christian Europe, 20th-century pluralistic America and 25th-century who-knows-what-or-where are all unique historical and existential moments which may call forth vastly different, and even mutually contradictory, conclusions, all drawn from the same Jewish texts, but read by different readers. Neither all Orthodox respondents nor all Reform respondents arrive at identical decisions as a group.[3] Orthodox communities follow the opinion of those authorities who are popularly esteemed as being <u>gedolei hador</u>, the halakhic giants of their generation. Reform communities have known our giants also -- notably, Rabbi Solomon Freehof -- but in general, these days, we prefer the wisdom of a responsa committee that meets like a supreme court to discuss matters as a group.

In other words, there is no alternative to the awesome but enlightening recognition that responsibility for our decisions cannot be displaced from our shoulders onto our texts. Only metaphorically do texts actually "speak" to us. We may hear them "say" something, but our hearing and their speaking are two very different matters indeed. We shall discover, therefore, that in the issues pertinent to non-Jews' participating in Jewish life-cycle ceremonies, we do not all hear the texts saying the same thing; we shall have to live with a certain amount of inconsistency between one congregation and another, and even between one case and another, which may be similar in some ways, but sufficiently different in others to prompt different conclusions from us. Life is not always as tidy as we should like it to be.

A Review of Reform Halakhic Precedents
Both Solomon Freehof and the CCAR's Committee on Responsa chaired by Walter Jacob have addressed the question of non-Jews participating in life cycle-ceremonies.[4]

In 1969, Rabbi Freehof was asked about a non-Jewish stepfather "who has adopted the child and been truly a father to the boy. It seems wrong to keep him from participating as father in the Bar Mitzvah ceremony of the son. What may or may not a Christian stepfather do in the ceremony?" Freehof noted some ritual acts and words that a Christian can do or say in good conscience -- such as being called to the Torah, which has sacred significance for Christians too, since "the Bible is sacred to Jews and Christians alike." But he distinguishes also a category of words and actions that Christians presumably cannot perform or recite without compromising themselves -- such as saying the standard Torah benediction which affirms, "who has chosen us ... and given us Torah." Being neither a Jew-by-Birth, nor a Jew-by-Choice, "this stepfather cannot truthfully recite the blessing," Freehof concluded, so he suggested rewording the blessing with a more universalistic affirmation, such as, "Praised be Thou... Who has given His sacred law unto all His [sic] children...."

What was an anomaly for Freehof in 1969 became commonplace for Reform Jews by 1979, so that the CCAR's Committee on Education that year asked a general question of its Committee on Responsa: "To what extent may non-Jews participate in a Jewish public service?" Responding for his committee, Rabbi Walter Jacob sided with Freehof's dichotomy between things which non-Jews can legitimately express without compromise and those they cannot. After a very positive and broad-ranging introductory summary of what, in fact, non-Jews have regularly been invited to do, even in traditional circles that preceded the rise of Reform Judaism, he concluded, "We have gone much further than any generation before our time, by permitting non-Jews a larger role in our public services; this is part of a more open and friendly interreligious attitude which the Reform movement has encouraged and led. Yet, these steps have remained within definite limits. We have not included non-Jews...in the essential elements of the service."

Thus, Rabbi Jacob urges that non-Jews be allowed to participate in three categories of liturgical act or speech:

1. Anything that does not require specific statements from them, i.e., by standing and silently witnessing whatever is taking place (e.g., as a member of a wedding party or as a pallbearer);
2. The recitation of special prayers added to the service at non-liturgical community-wide services, commemorations, and celebrations (Thanksgiving, etc.);
3. The recitation of prayers for special family occasions (such as Bar/Bat Mitzvah of children raised as Jews, at a wedding or funeral, etc.).

But they would not be permitted to act as <u>sheliach tzibur</u> (the leader of prayers),[5] or (as in the case before us) to recite the Sabbath <u>Kiddush</u> or bless Sabbath candles, for example, even if it was normally the custom for parents to do so on the eve of their children's Bar/Bat Mitzvah.

In 1983, Rabbi Jacob's committee returned to the issue, this time to define "Non-Jewish Participation in a Bar/Bat Mitzvah Service." The case involved a Jewish mother and a Christian father. The questioner wondered, "Are there any limits to participation?"

Obviously, the committee had already staked out its general direction in the 1979 responsum, but it felt it wise now to elaborate on what its general guidelines there might mean in this specific life-cycle event, which has returned to Reform Jewish practice with surprising vitality, emerging as the symbolic gesture <u>par excellence</u> by which parents demonstrate that they have "done right" by their children and by Judaism, in that they have seen to their child's education as a Jew, and passed along the Jewish heritage to the next generation.[6]

Though continuous with prior rulings, this committee's statement of 1983 proves rather surprising. Non-Jewish parents are forbidden to "lead the major segments of our service, to proclaim the traditional <u>berakhot</u> or phrases such as, `Who has commanded us,' or `Who has chosen us.'" Further, they are not "to remove the Torah from the ark and hand it to the Bar/Bat Mitzvah," since this ritual action "is frequently accompanied by a statement indicating the transmission of the Jewish tradition from one generation to another." Non-Jewish parents are limited to addressing their children with "private words or prayers at an appropriate point during the Torah service," and, in the opinion of only a minority of the committee members, to lead "some specific psalms or responsive readings" from the early part of the service prior to the <u>barekhu</u> (the formal call to communal prayer). Surprisingly, Freehof's early advocacy of rewriting standard blessings so as to universalize their content, thus rendering them appropriate for non-Jewish speakers was held now by only a minority of one! The rest of the committee recommended, in summary, "that participation of non-Jews in a Bar/Bat Mitzvah ceremony be sharply restricted."

Clearly, at least in tone, and even in content, compared to its precedents, this 1983 statement is less generously disposed to non-

Jewish participation. Whereas Freehof's initial responsum of 1969 was <u>inclusive</u> in intent, trying to find ways in which a non-Jewish stepfather might participate without moral compromise in his son's service of Bar Mitzvah, here both questioner and respondents take an <u>exclusive</u> perspective, seeking the limits to what such parents may do. Moreover, whereas Freehof's early responsum addressed the issue as a conflict for the Christian parent -- what might the stepfather say without personally perjuring himself by asserting a doctrine of Jewish faith with which he could not agree -- the committee of 1983 looked at the issue more from the perspective of the congregation at prayer, and the integrity of the service of worship which they, as Jews, were attending.

Here we have a clear instance of the importance of "reading strategy" to which I referred above. Freehof's question of his texts was how the service could legitimately be changed so as to allow a non-Jew to participate without personal anguish. The 1983 committee's question to the same Jewish texts was how to limit such participation, so as to protect the legitimate interests of Jewish tradition and the Jewish community celebrating it in its Shabbat liturgy.

The fact is that even Rabbi Freehof had changed perspective by the 1980s. In 1980, Freehof was asked expressly whether "an unconverted Gentile...may bless the Sabbath candles...[or] recite the <u>Kiddush</u>."[7] Since the Sabbath is a sign of God's covenant with Israel (Exodus 31:16), Freehof decides that "it would be contrary to the spirit of tradition for a Gentile to perform such parts of the service as constitute the special announcements of the Jewish-covenant Sabbath." Moreover, since the Christian Church once publicly abolished the Sabbath in favor of adopting Sunday as the Lord's Day, Freehof avers that "the simple human fact is that the Jewish Sabbath can have no sacred meaning to a Christian." Again, compared with the initial words penned by the same author in 1969, we have a responsum with a subtle change in reading strategy. Though continuous with the earlier opinion, it is not couched in the same spirit. The 1980 opinion is defensive in tone, protecting "the spirit of tradition" against incursions by well-meaning congregations and/or parents who overstep the bounds. "The motive to make a Gentile member feel at home so as not to alienate the family is in general a good one," Freehof says, "but to have a Gentile announce the coming of the Jewish Sabbath to a Jewish congregation is contrary to the spirit of Jewish tradition."

As in all serious religious dilemmas, we have contrary goods being weighed in the balance against each other. Both non-Jewish parents (and their families) and Jewish congregations (including Jews-by-Choice) require understanding and more than a little sympathy as they struggle to protect their own legitimate interests at a life-cycle event that may already be sufficiently overly charged with emotional tensions as to tempt rabbis, ritual committees, and (above all) Bar/Bat Mitzvah parents to wish that Bar/Bat Mitzvah had never been invented![8]

Some Limits to the Argument

The sum total of what we have seen in Reform statements on the subject has a certain consistency.

1. Non-Jews may not say anything -- e.g., "who has chosen us..." -- the content of which presupposes that the speaker is Jewish.

2. Non-Jews may not do anything -- e.g., passing down the Torah as a sign of one's own Jewish heritage being conveyed, or even just removing the Torah from the ark, if that gesture will be interpreted as part of the ritual of heritage conveyance -- the symbolic meaning of which presupposes that the person doing it is Jewish.

3. Non-Jews may not lead the congregation in the standard prayers that constitute Jewish liturgy's core -- the shema for example, or benedictions.

4. The grounds for all of the above are both the religious integrity of the non-Jew and of the congregation gathered in worship.

Still, it is hard to read the documents without some nagging problems regarding the limits of the argument on which these conclusions are based. I will mention a few here, not because I necessarily disagree (or agree) with the consensus I have recorded, but because it is important to see that arguments are never totally objective. There is always room for good people to disagree on an issue as complex as this. Halakhic thinking is a necessary part of the process by which Jews determine their position on anything, but Halakhah conceptualized as an objective reading of texts is insufficient.

How does Freehof know for sure, for example, that "the Jewish Sabbath can have no sacred meaning to a Christian"? Actually, the trend in Christianity lately is just the reverse: to take the Jewish Sabbath more seriously, as part of a Christian's total biblical heritage. That does not mean that Saturday has the same sanctity for a Christian as it does for a Jew. But it need not have "no sacred meaning at all." Besides, in the context of a Jewish community in which non-Jews have taken a stand as parents of Jewish children, surely it is unlikely that they have no feeling for the Sabbath at all. There is a certain presumption here to the effect that since they have not chosen to become Jewish, they must not yet have decided to affirm what Jews affirm. That may or may not be the case. People convert for all sorts of reasons, just as they hesitate to do so for an equally large number of reasons, including such things as how their parents will react, or how certain they want to be before they take a step into another faith that is rightly seen as incredibly consequential and even irreversible. We err if we see this as an all-or-nothing thing, as if one is either wholly a Jew or wholly not one. Actually most Jews-by-Choice experience a lengthy process through which they slowly become Jews, and at some point along the way, they opt for the ceremony which publicly affirms that process. Without actual consultation with the person involved, who is to say in advance what a given person can or cannot affirm at any given point along the way, and whether the non-Jewish parent may not be able to say that this is indeed his/her Shabbat?

The same objection can be raised regarding any given liturgical text -- such as "who has chosen us..." or "commanded us..." -- the words of which seem to imply that the speaker is one of us -- that is, a Jew. A text's implications, however, are sometimes a reader's inferences. Perhaps some non-Jews can speak of being "chosen" too; certainly they ought theoretically to be able to say they are "commanded." Not for nothing have they decided to raise their children as Jews, to guarantee their Jewish education, and to nurture their Jewish souls. While some may do this out of convenience or out of respect for their Jewish spouse, others may well do it out of religious conviction, arising from the way they see themselves standing before God.

Moreover, why can't a Christian "announce the coming of the Jewish Sabbath to a Jewish congregation," and is that, in fact, the only thing that the Kiddush and the candle-lighting blessing do? For a long time now, some of our congregations have hired non-Jewish singers as choir members and soloists, and until 1985, no one objected when they sang the words in question.[9] The difference was, of course, that a non-Jewish parent is assumed actually to be praying with us, while a hired soloist prays for us. But in so far as we see the reader merely announcing Shabbat's arrival, why should non-Jewish parents who have freely demonstrated at least some affinity for Judaism in their decision to bring their children to this Bar/Bat Mitzvah point in their lives be more disadvantaged than a soloist who comes here only as a matter of professional interest? If our concern is announcing Shabbat, then, we have the precedent of the soloists, and if our concern is the theological content of prayers that affirm the speaker is "one of us," we should at least ask the parents whom we encounter in this role what they think -- not what we think -- they can affirm in good conscience, since, perhaps, despite their decision not (or not yet) to undergo the formal conversion ritual, they are far enough along the road to Jewish identity that they can make the particular affirmation that the prayer in question contains.

In any of these arguments, I see no way to arrive at conclusions so obvious that they defy criticism. Deciding Halakhah is a case of reading texts; and reading texts is an ambiguous undertaking, fraught with variant readings. Moreover, we have by and large been considering the legal texts (the Reform responsa and their precedents) whence we get our guidance. But there is another kind of texts here: the liturgical texts which prompt the discussion in the first place. Even if the final Halakhic decision were to go against non-Jewish reading of all these liturgical texts in so far as they constitute theological statements about our Shabbat, God's choosing us, and the like, it may be that prayer is more than theology, and the act of worship more than the process of declaring one's faith in this or that doctrine. Before reaching a final conclusion on what we should do, we have to consider what liturgists call the multivocality of liturgical texts, and their function as performative language.

<u>Liturgical Texts: Ambiguous and Performative</u>
What does a liturgical text "mean"? On the face of it, a text means whatever its words say. On the other hand, we already saw how a text's meaning is at best slippery, dependent in large part on what we called reader-strategy, so the words may mean different things to different readers. Still, there are limits to what a strategy can do. Some strategies are more "deviant" than others. It would be hard to imagine reading <u>Hamlet</u> as a comedy, for example, or <u>Death of a Salesman</u> as a farce. Similarly, our prayers have some objectivity: they are not about just anything we wish them to be. Their verbal meaning may be elastic, but elasticity has its limits beyond which it breaks. Eventually, we come up with some publicly recognized sense of the boundaries within which people may legitimately offer interpretations of a prayer's content, but outside of which interpretations are judged unacceptable.

If a "deviant" reader doesn't agree with the consensus, he or she tries to convince a reading public that the reading in question is not as deviant as they thought. Thus, Reform Judaism championed readings of traditional sacred texts that their Orthodox opponents judged deviant, but Reformers persevered until a Reform community asserted successfully that their reading was not deviant at all. From this perspective, Orthodoxy and Reform are two reading communities reading the same texts (and therefore both Jewish), but with different strategies, and a different consensus on the boundaries of licit interpretation. A similar example comes from first-century Christianity which interpreted Jewish texts beyond the bounds of what rabbis considered acceptable. As long as they read Jewish texts, they were still Jewish. But unlike Reform Judaism, Christians then developed their own novel set of texts which displaced the centrality of Jewish texts. Only at that point did they leave Judaism. So every religious community has its own set of texts, along with various sub-groups who offer competing readings of them. The texts of the Jewish people include a body of prayers that Reform Jews generally agree to interpret according to a consensus that makes us uniquely Reform.

It is this verbal meaning, or manifest content of the prayers, that was reflected in the responsa at which we looked. The authors noted, for instance, that the prayers in question "meant" that God had chosen us and commanded us; that God had sanctified a Shabbat that we greet, announce, and observe; and so forth. It was the logical inconsistency (they thought) of a non-Jew saying these things and meaning those meanings that led them to reject the non-Jew's participation in this or that part of the service.

But it now turns out that texts have more than one meaning. Any given reading community must work within the reading consensus which defines them as a community (that is, we all read our texts with a reader strategy consonant with the fact that we are Reform Jews), but within that consensus, we may each posit a somewhat different meaning to our texts.

Moreover, this textual ambiguity, if we can call it that, is particularly manifest in communal liturgical texts, which are composed in such a way that they unify many individual worshippers together through their act of praying as a group. In order to do that, liturgical texts tend to speak with deliberate vagueness, lest any particular worshipper's meaning be so substantiated, while rival reading of other worshippers be implicitly denied, to the point where group solidarity is threatened. Our prayers are often poetic, for example, or they use ancient imagery which is hard to pin down exactly. They move rapidly from topic to topic, rather than spelling out the theological suppositions and complete argument behind any particular topic. They mention things like chosenness, commandments, Shabbat or a messianic age, but never actually define what they mean. And they use formulaic language -- such as the introduction to blessings -- which allows us to read rapidly through them without giving too much thought to what each and every word means. (Barukh atah Adonai..., for example, functions as if it were one long word, barukhatahadonai, said quickly without conscious thought, so that worshippers need not ponder what it means to call God atah or to attribute to God a quality known as barukh). In other words, good liturgy is always somewhat vague liturgy, evocative of conceptualizations in general, but falling short of the kind of rigorous definitions and development of thought that mark arguments in law, study in the classroom, and other similar linguistic enterprises in which we participate from time to time.

Since liturgical texts are purposefully ambiguous, alluding to many different possible readings at a given time, we can say that liturgical texts are multivocal -- that is, they speak with many voices all at once.

The multivocality of prayer language lies behind my claim earlier that we might consider asking non-Jews what they mean by a given liturgical prayer. As non-Jewish members in the Jewish community, they stand mid-way between two alternative reading publics, representing, respectively, the Christian consensus and the Jewish consensus. It may be that on any given issue, they find themselves reading liturgical texts with a Jewish reading strategy. The same question of what we mean by a text should be put to ourselves as well. Regardless of what the "experts" tell us a text means, we may say it in our prayers with other meanings in mind. At the very least, discussion of meanings makes for a fascinating process of belief clarification; and in the end, it soon becomes clear whether some non-Jews, no non-Jews, or all non-Jews might be able to say the prayer in question, and why.

Prayer ambiguity (or multivocality) is only the first liturgical consideration that we have to add to the halakhic considerations detailed above. Even more important is a second characteristic of liturgical language: the fact that its verbal meaning, or manifest content of the prayers, is just one kind of meaning that a prayer has, and not the most important one at that. If you ask people what a prayer means to them, you will often find that they do not even refer to its content. Instead they will say something like, "For me, that prayer asserts my solidarity with the Jewish people," or "My parents said that prayer, so I say it; it is my connection to my past." People sometimes even recite prayers with which they disagree completely. Sometimes they are in Hebrew, so they do not have to face up to what the prayers mean. Other times, they sing them, so that they can relate positively to the melody while ignoring the content. Too much dissonance is hard to live with, so we "cheat" on translations, or provide paraphrases that let people read English versions (at least) of prayers that offer the chance of a positive interpretation. But prayer is not the same as study. Prayer is an act of identity formation, a ritual by which we assert the ultimacy of our lives among others committed to the same ultimacies, in a setting and in a manner that reinforces our faith in an ultimate being we call God. As such, prayer calls us to do many things that transcend the level of reading the content of sentences or paragraphs as if they were essays for our leisurely rational consideration, which we then accept as true or reject as false.

It is customary to speak of language doing different things. Sometimes, as in scientific treatises, it asserts truths, and then we judge it by whether what it says is true or false. But sometimes it does something else. When the rabbi marries two people, and concludes, "I declare you husband and wife," no one wonders whether it is really true that they are husband and wife; if the conditions are right -- the rabbi is serious, this is not just a dress rehearsal, and so forth -- the rabbi's saying it makes it so. When the saying of something makes it so (like: "I bet you fifty dollars," which establishes a bet), we say that the language "performs its task." It makes no sense now to ask, "But is it true?" Rather, we ask whether the task got done right, whether I anted up the fifty dollars, say, or whether the rabbi giggled through the ceremony so that everyone knew the wedding was not for real. When language functions to perform a task, we say it is <u>performative</u>.

Ritualized language is very highly performative, and only slightly informational. Its truth or falsity is generally not even an issue. People engage in it not so much to tell truths as to perform tasks. Among other things, they praise or thank God, tell sacred tales, affirm age-old hopes, assure each other that life is meaningful, commit themselves to certain behavior in their life outside the sanctuary, and order their spiritual and ethical priorities.[10] Worship thus tells few truths; but it functions performatively to bring something about. It creates community, expresses faith, raises consciousness, marks sacred time, and so forth. The question regarding non-Jews' participation in Jewish rituals is therefore only partly dependent upon the "truths" that they may or may not say with a clear conscience. More important are the performative meanings to the prayers in question, the tasks that liturgical units are intended to perform, and whether those meanings will be undermined if a non-Jew says the prayers that bring them about.

Take the act of lighting the candles Friday night. The verbal content asserts that God commanded us to kindle Sabbath lights. But Bar/Bat Mitzvah parents say the blessing with their own performative meanings in mind. Perhaps the meaning of that liturgical staple is their assertion that they have raised their children to this significant moment, and that they stand before the community proud of their accomplishment. Consider even the handing down of tradition in the ritual by which the Torah is passed from grandparents to parents to the Bar/Bat Mitzvah child. There, it is the action, not the words, that speak loudest. I can imagine that some non-Jewish parents who raise their child as a Jew, despite their own non-Jewish background, might well want to participate in such a ceremony, not as a sign that their own heritage is being delivered from their parents to their child, but as an affirmation of the value of the Jewish tradition that they cared so much to nurture in their offspring. If they wished to, why couldn't a non-Jewish parent hold the Torah scroll and hand it to his or her child as a vivid symbol of the way he or she took Jewish tradition into the home, inculcated it in the child, and now watches that child accept the Torah as his or her life-long spiritual guide?

Searching Out Meanings

I make no claim that the responsa surveyed above are wrong. On the contrary, they hold a great deal of wisdom. There must be areas where any group's sacred service has to emanate from fully identified members of the group in question. The responsa over the years have helped us focus our attention on some of the halakhic considerations that should go into deciding what those areas are.

I have tried, however, to expand the purview of the discussion, to include considerations of how we read texts in general, how non-Jewish parents are just as conflicted over this issue as the Jews who determine policy in the synagogues which they join, and how liturgical texts in particular take on meanings beyond their officially sanctioned verbal content.

The determination of what we really mean in our liturgies is an ongoing process. Rather than pass congregational rules based on the putative single meaning that a given text's content is said to contain, we should engage in an open exploration of the many meanings, verbal and otherwise, that our liturgical actions and words denote. Why do we light Shabbat candles? What does the Hebrew blessing and its melody convey to us? Is it important for the Bar/Bat Mitzvah parent to light candles at the bimah? If so, why? What would we think if we saw someone refuse to do it? What would we think if we noted a non-Jewish parent who did it? And so forth.

A series of such questions would emerge regarding each of our disputed liturgical acts and prayers, if we were only to ask of each other and ourselves: "What meaning do you see in such and such?" The halakhic literature summarized above would be central to our attaining the educational level from which serious questions can proceed; and our honest and personal analysis of our own experience of acting out the prayers every Shabbat would inform us of additional layers of meaning that we wish to consider. Knowing that each of us is an active reader of our texts, and that reader strategies are inherent to the reading task, we would be prepared to hear our friends in the discussion say things that we would never have come upon ourselves. By listening to each other carefully, we would develop a consensus, as well as boundaries beyond which readings of meaning would be held to deviate from that which makes us a coherent reading public called Reform Jews.

Finally, there is the step by which we operationalize our consensus in our dealing with non-Jews who wish to join our worship as active participants at their family's life-cycle events. Knowing the meanings we see in liturgical actions and words, we will know where non-Jews too may play active roles in our rituals. If a candle-lighting blessing "means" that its speaker affirms his or her full membership in this covenanted community that now performs a commanded task of kindling Sabbath lights, it may follow that non-Jews may under no circumstances say that prayer -- neither non-Jewish parents, nor non-Jewish choir members. If, however, that blessing functions in a symbolic way to affirm the spiritual worth of a parent who has brought his or her child to Jewish adulthood, or if it publicly symbolizes that parent's worth to the child, then we may insist that all parents say it, especially a non-Jewish parent who had an easy option of denying this child's Jewish education, but did not do so. Alternatively, if the blessing means all of the above, we might find ourselves wishing that non-Jewish parents could say it, and then, unable to grant that, but unwilling also to embarrass them before their children (who might not understand why their parents alone are refused permission to participate publicly), we might revise the Friday night ritual so that no parents say that blessing, or so that it is said in such a way that everyone can say it (perhaps the kindling is done by the parents, but the blessing is said by the congregation.)

I mean to offer no single solution to fit every instance. We will have to explore our meanings together, content with the recognition that there will be considerable diversity from congregation to congregation, and even from case to case, as non-Jewish parents too join the dialogue, some of them opting for one thing and others for another. They too must wrestle with the question of what a proffered opportunity for ritual involvement means in their consciousness. Sometimes they will ask to be included, and we will say no; sometimes we will invite their inclusion, and they will say no: all because of how we or they read the sacred text of the liturgy that has room somewhere for us all, even though it is not always immediately clear to us where.

This article also appears in <u>Journal of Reform Judaism</u>, Summer 1990.

NOTES

1. For full discussion of <u>Worship in Common</u> and <u>Indigenous Worship with Guests</u>, see Lawrence A. Hoffman, "Worship in Common: Babel or Mixed Multitude? "<u>Crosscurrents: Journal of the Association for Religion and Intellectual Life</u> 40:1 (Spring:1990).

2. See Joel Roth, <u>The Halakhic Process: A Systemic Analysis</u> (New York: Jewish Theological Seminary of America, 1986), Ch. 1. Historical sources lacking legally formal recognition by the law itself "are not accounted legally significant by the system" (p.5).

3. See Louis Newman, "Woodchoppers and Respirators: The Problem of Interpretation in Contemporary Jewish Ethics," <u>Modern Judaism</u> 10 (1990).

4. Cf. "Gentile Stepfather at Bar Mitzvah," in Solomon Freehof, <u>Current Reform Responsa</u> (Cincinnati: Hebrew Union College Press, 1969), p. 91-93; "Participation of Non-Jews in Jewish Public Service (1979)," in Walter Jacob, ed., <u>American Reform Responsa: Jewish Questions, Rabbinic Answers</u> (New York: Central Conference of American Rabbis, 1983); and "Non-Jewish Participation in Bar/Bat Mitzvah Service," in Walter Jacob, <u>Contemporary American Reform Responsa</u> (New York: Central Conference of American Rabbis, 1987). See also related responsa cited at the conclusion of "Participation of Non-Jews in Jewish Public Service." p. 24.

5. The standard argument against a non-Jew leading a Jewish congregation in the standard order of prayer revolves about the rabbinic principle according to which the leader of prayer is a <u>sheliach tzibur</u> -- literally, "the agent of the congregation." It is the leader's job to represent the congregation before God, to which end the congregation vests the leader with the legal right of agency. But the rabbis also maintained that in matters of <u>mitzvot</u>, people may commission an agent to represent them in a <u>mitzvah</u> only if that agent already bears personal responsibility for doing the <u>mitzvah</u> in question. Hence, non-Jews may freely join a congregation in its prayers, and may even lead Jews in prayers that are not strictly speaking "commanded as <u>mitzvot</u>" -- such as benedictions at a civic gathering, or prayers of thanksgiving at a Thanksgiving Day Service in common -- but

they may not function at a normative daily service as the congregation's agent, or sheliach tzibur. The committee's responsum does not expressly link its decision to this traditional argument, but merely summarizes the decision to prohibit non-Jewish participation in leading standard prayers as universal practice.

6. Recent sociological literature sees Bar/Bat Mitzvah as a social marker for the whole family, a rite of passage for parents also, "the earliest moment in a family's life when it can publicly demonstrate what status it has achieved...the paramount, large-scale, public display of group identity" (Izumi Sato and Leonard Plotnicov, "Pittsburgh Middle-Class Jewish Families: Structural Assimilation Tested Through Bar/Bat Mitzvahs," Contemporary Jewry 10:1 [1989], pp. 61-62). As a symbolic event, the Bar/Bat Mitzvah surely means many things, the public demonstration of status among them; but particularly following the Holocaust, even the civil religious values rate intergenerational continuity very high (see Jonathan S. Woocher, Sacred Survival: The Civil Religion of America's Jews [Bloomington and Indianapolis: Indiana University Press, 1986]), so that there is reason to impute also this "religious" rationale to parental concern that their children participate in at least this one act of being a full-fledged Jew.

7. Solomon Freehof, New Reform Responsa (Cincinnati: Hebrew Union College Press, 1980), pp. 33-36.

8. For a sobering view on the extent to which Bar/Bat Mitzvah really does bring out enormous amounts of family anxiety, see Edwin Friedman, "Bar Mitzvah When the Parents Are No Longer Partners," Journal of Reform Judaism 28:2 (Spring 1981). His views are relevant to every Bar/Bat Mitzvah, regardless of family constellation, in that Bar/Bat Mitzvah brings family together with unresolved conflicts, replaying old issues fraught with unconscious implications. Particularly hazardous are situations where family stress has built up because of non-traditional marriage decisions -- the case of divorce (for Friedman), but also (of interest to us) mixed marriages that may still retain more that a residue of family conflict between the two parents' families of origin, or between each of their sets of parents (on one hand) and themselves and their spouses (on the other).

9. See "Non Jewish Voices in Congregational Choir," in Jacob, ed., Contemporary American Reform Responsa, pp. 195-196. The responsum urges the use of Jewish voices whenever possible, because of the additional kavanah (prayerful intent) that would be gained. But, following the guidelines in the earlier responsum on non-Jews in general, non-Jewish singers are permitted to lead only liturgical rubrics that are not central

to the service. "All public services must be lead by Jews, and it would be inappropriate for a non-Jew to lead a service from the pulpit." On the other hand, the non-Jewish choir member is allowed to sing with the congregation -- precisely what usually happens with regard to both the candle-lighting blessing and the Sabbath <u>Kiddush</u>, which are permitted to non-Jewish choir members here, but not to non-Jewish parents of Bar/Bat Mitzvah children.

10. For a discussion of the many ways that words "perform" in prayer, see Lawrence A. Hoffman, <u>The Art of Public Prayer: Not for Clergy Only</u> (Washington D.C.: Pastoral Press, 1988), p. 225-242.

DISCUSSION QUESTIONS:

1. What does the author mean by "the grand experiment in pluralism that may in the long run turn out to be North America's greatest contribution to human history?" What have been the positive and negative effects of pluralism on the Jewish people?

2. The author notes that a non-Jewish parent "will necessarily be thrust into a severe conflict" in regard to participation in various aspects of life-cycle ceremonies. Do you agree? What is the basis of this conflict?

3. The author makes an argument regarding "the ultimate non-authority" of Jewish sources. Describe Reform perspective(s) about religious authority.

4. What is your reaction to Rabbi Hoffman's statement that "there is no alternative to the awesome but enlightening recognition that responsibility for our decisions cannot be displaced from our shoulders onto our texts?"

5. In reviewing Reform responsa precedents, the author traces the history of attitudes in the responsa toward the inclusion of non-Jews in worship. To what do you attribute the changes in perspective that he describes? What has been the impact of the participation of increasing numbers of non-Jews in the temple on the attitudes of the Reform community?

6. Rabbi Hoffman states in a footnote that a Bar/Bat Mitzvah is the earliest moment in a family's life cycle when it can publicly demonstrate the status it has achieved." To what kind of status is the author referring? Why is an understanding of this concept important in helping us to understand the feelings of families as they approach significant life-cycle events?

7. Do Jews always believe what they are reading in the prayerbook?

8. The author suggests that our texts "have more than one meaning." How does the notion of a Reform Jewish community relate to the notion of interpretive freedom in liturgy? Are common beliefs and/or interpretations necessary for the strength and well-being of the Reform Jewish community? Of K'lal Yisrael?

9. Are there some ritual acts which should be reserved for Jews only? If so, what involvement in ritual is appropriate or inappropriate for non-Jews? On what do you base your opinion?

10. Rabbi Priesand's article (which is the last essay in this section) suggests that her congregation sought changes in their constitution "to adopt a policy that would protect and preserve the Jewishness of our congregation." According to Rabbi Hoffman, is the notion of "Jewishness" open to interpretation? What is your view?

Some Comments on Lawrence A. Hoffman's Essay

by
Rabbi W. Gunther Plaut
Senior Scholar
Holy Blossom Temple
Toronto, Ontario

Two disclaimers first. One, what follows is my own personal reaction, and not that of the Responsa Committee, which has developed its own way of arriving at responsa. Its members may agree with my conclusions and then again, they may not. Two, I am not about to give my own teshuvah (response) to the questions with which Rabbi Hoffman deals.

His essay sparkles with all the qualities for which he has become so widely known: his mastery of liturgy, his generous approach to the thinking of others, his clarity of thought and expression; and as always, he instructs us about the deeper layers of liturgy. At the same time his approach leaves me somewhat uneasy, for it deals not only with the nature of liturgy but also, by implication, with the way Reform responsa might or should be created.

By their nature, Reform teshuvot begin with Halakhah and then proceed to the understanding which Reform Judaism brings to the tradition. In the matter of non-Jewish participation in our life-cycle liturgy we also take into consideration the sensibilities of the Gentile participants. They find themselves in an essentially alien environment, and we in turn desire to make them feel as comfortable as we possibly can, given our own limitations. "As in all serious religious dilemmas, we have contrary goods being weighed in the balance against each other," Hoffman reminds us. Just how to arrive at a proper balance is the question to which he addresses himself.

In his words, "deciding Halakhah is a case of reading texts; and reading texts is an ambiguous undertaking, fraught with various readings." Quite so, but there are limits; the Halakhah defines them and the Reform tradition subjects them to further scrutiny.

Now it is true that the most explicit of mitzvot have their ifs and buts built into them. Thus, Lo tirtzach (do not murder) is an apodictic rule which seems clear enough, but then again, one may kill during a war or in self-defense. But how, for instance, is self-defense to be defined? Police officers acting during periods of high stress and danger can attest to that difficulty. Still, the difficulty of definition does not obviate the need to make a judgment, which must pass the test of credibility and should not open the door any wider than necessary, so that there be no disregard of the basic rule itself. I am sure that Hoffman would agree.

Jewish liturgy has its own rules and structures and -- as Hoffman has taught us -- is both ambiguous and performative. Yet even liturgy has a limited number of ways to understand it. There are built-in limits, as the first-century Christians (to whom Hoffman refers) found out.

Hoffman bases much of his exposition on reading liturgy as "purposefully ambiguous, alluding to many different possible readings at a given time," which makes them "multivocal -- that is, they speak with many voices all at once." Here I come to my first question: How does he know that liturgy is purposefully ambiguous? Liturgical texts, to use his terminology, may indeed be multivocal, but is this not the result of many people hearing the liturgy and coming to it with their own power to understand? Is our liturgy so planned as to elicit multivocality by design? Does it not rather derive its ambiguity from the fact that congregants understand it differently because of their humanness rather than because of the authors' intent? The Midrash, applying this experience to the revelation at Sinai, says that God spoke with one voice but the Israelites heard the words in different ways.

This points to an important difference. We may create liturgy to be purposefully ambiguous and have on occasion done so. But on the whole, our liturgy attempts to be reasonably straightforward, except that -- because it consists of words -- it lends itself to various or even many understandings. To take but one example: the word God may be interpreted by the congregation in a multiplicity of ways, which does not, however, concede that the authors of the liturgy were willing to have God mean a life force that has no relationship to Israel -- even though some hearers may interpret the text in that fashion.

Hoffman's second consideration deals with another aspect of the meaning of prayer, namely, its performative quality. "Ritualized language is very highly performative.... It creates community, expresses faith, raises consciousness, marks sacred time, and so forth," he reminds us and at the same time emphasizes that, to him, this is the more important quality. Thus the transmission of a sefer Torah during a Bar/Bat Mitzvah ceremony is a performative act that speaks loudly to those participating in it. I would agree. But Bar/Bat Mitzvah ceremonies are not only for the family, they are also ritual dramas performed before the congregants who are shutafim (participants) in the observance. Should we not aim at having the essence of the celebration create as common a basis for everyone as we can possibly do? There will still be the individual with his/her own reaction patterns, but hopefully there will also be a large common ground. And that common ground, with all the respect we have for the non-Jewish parent's sensitivity, must first and foremost be the way in which a Jewish congregation expresses its love for God, Torah and Israel.

Hoffman speaks admirably and sensitively of the many layers of meaning that Gentile parents bring to the occasion. However, unless the rabbi has carefully instructed the congregation in advance, the focus on non-Jewish needs may become unwittingly a divisive rather than a uniting factor. Hoffman is aware of this possibility, and the solutions which he proposes in his final sentences point to that problem.

This bring me to the matter of a <u>teshuvah</u>. Hoffman, basing himself on the liturgy's multivocality and performative qualities, argues that each case must be treated separately, because questions emerge "regarding each of our liturgical acts and prayers." If that be so, what guidance could a teshuvah give except to point out that there really cannot be a general rule? The general rule represents the <u>kelal</u> vis-a-vis the individual, and I for one would not grant the latter unlimited sway.

I therefore feel uneasy with Hoffman's conclusion, which seems to dispense with congregational guidelines and instead raises the exception to the level of principle. Would this not be an invitation to a further extension of <u>hefkerut</u>, (confusion) which already plays havoc with Reform Jewish life and which, I am sure, Hoffman deplores? To be sure, he deals only with a very specific case in liturgy, but I fear that the approach he advocates has unintended implications. It would have the ambiguity and multivocality of liturgy determine how responsa would function, when in fact they have their own framework.

Responsa are designed to set perimeters for Jewish life, and end most of the time with a "Yes"or "No". To be sure, in Reform responsa there will usually be a good deal of discretion and a tendency toward leniency and exceptions. The very question to which Hoffman's essay addresses itself bespeaks our openness to, and consideration for the non-Jewish partners in the ceremony, a scenario quite inconceivable in Conservative or Orthodox synagogues. Still, it is a Reform <u>Jewish</u> congregation before whom the drama is played out, and that congregation must remain the ultimate focus of our concern.

There will of need be many a "maybe," but liberalism is not thereby defined. The nature of our Committee on Responsa, as I understand it, is to begin by asking what Halakhah has to say about a problem and then proceed to inquire whether there is a Reform Jewish principle that would compel us to disagree. If there is not, we will reassert the conclusions upon which our tradition has based itself.[1]

---

[1] The answer at which we arrive is the result of a process in which all members of the Committee on Responsa participate, and if there is a minority of even one, that minority has the right to issue a separate dissent. In the short time of my incumbency this has not yet happened, but I am sure it will sooner or later.

To return to the question at hand. We respond to the person who asks the she'elah (question) by setting forth how we perceive our tradition to deal with this subject. With Hoffman, we would be alive to the multi-faceted nature of a worship service and its liturgical connotations. But I for one would also wish to have the limits marked out and have them explained with compassion and sensitivity. The integrity of our religious service demands no less.

****

This article also appears in Journal of Reform Judaism, Summer 1990.

W. Gunther Plaut is Senior Scholar at Holy Blossom Temple, Toronto and Chairman of the CCAR Committee on Responsa.

Jewish Life-Cycle Liturgy and Non-Jews

by
Rabbi Joseph B. Glaser
Executive Vice President
Central Conference of American Rabbis

The subject is, indeed, a challenge. But the challenge is more than an intellectual one, allowing wandering through uncharted speculations about intentions and significance for the participant and reading strategies. The challenge here is to the very validity of the Reform Jewish enterprise. Will our critics, both within and without, the serious ones, finally be right that in Reform Judaism, "anything goes"?

Rabbi Samuel E. Karff, CCAR President, 1989-91, has referred to this as a "boundary issue". Where do we draw the line? Do we draw lines? Can we really think of the Jewish sources as ultimately non-authoritative? Then there is no center for us -- except ourselves. "...There is no alternative to the awesome and enlightening recognition that responsibility for our decisions cannot be displaced from our shoulders onto our texts," quotes the discussion question exercise. This is a great Humanist proclamation, but we are not Humanists. We have a tradition - and we have a God. That is the center.

The time of life-cycle ceremonies is one fraught with emotional turbulence. It is made far more so by the existence of a non-Jewish parent, grandparent or other principal. Concern for the feelings of those people and their families, especially the Bar/Bat Mitzvah, is commendable, and we all share it. But can we abide that some seem to make an equation of the interests of the family at issue, on the one hand, and the demands of a stream of Judaism already beset with the problems and stresses of the vagueness and ambiguity necessarily characteristic of such a radical movement as ours?

Elsewhere in this document, we read that prayer and worship are for asserting the ultimacies of our lives. Unless we see that prayer and worship are for communion with the transcendent, and that only God is ultimate, we have, again, only a Humanist position, but one from which it is easy to jump to the conclusion that a non-Jew may determine in his or her own mind (for the day, anyway) that it is all right to be "chosen" and thus to recite the Torah blessings and/or to hand down the Torah "from generation to generation" and/or to recite the benediction over the Sabbath candles, "who has sanctified us by Your commandments and commanded us...."

Elsewhere in this document, there is assigned to worship a primary function of "creating community". It is difficult to understand how this could be when, on the other hand, there is asserted the primacy of private meanings and significance and strategy in the mind of each worshipper. This does not bode well for a sense of community, particularly when the very consensus as to Jewish identity itself is so confused by the participation of non-Jews in deeply essentially Jewish prayers and rituals. We can speculate to no end about why the non-Jew is not able or willing to convert or what is in his or her mind as s/he performs the rituals at issue here, and be intimidated by such judgmental adjectives as "exclusive," "defensive" and "less generous."

We can, and certainly should, be very sensitive to, and concerned about, the feelings of the children involved in these situations. And I cannot help but think that these children are a lot more conscious of the reality that we give them credit for. They know that for one reason or another, the parent is not totally committed to Judaism. I suspect that they may sense a whiff of hypocrisy, and may well prefer a more honest acting out of the parental role. I also suspect that we have here at work the same hyperemotional factors that exist in the controversy over rabbinic officiation at intermarriage ceremonies: guilt, appearance, appeasement of parents and grandparents.

The inference to be drawn from the accomodationist stance is simply this: a non-Jew will make the decision as to what is important and appropriate within a Jewish service. The obvious problem with this is not ameliorated by warnings that "we err if we see this as an all or nothing thing as if one is either wholly a Jew or wholly not one." Indeed, that only compounds the problem. If we are to survive as a movement, we must have some kind of a base, some sort of sure footing. For this to be provided, we have to know who is committed to the basics of Judaism, so that when they speak and serve and vote in our highly democratic institutional structures, when they represent us, we will know that they are doing so Jewishly. To allow for less is to eliminate authenticity and put integrity at severe risk.

There is a line. Its name is Commitment.

Non-Jews at Jewish Celebrations

by
Rabbi Harvey J. Fields
Wilshire Boulevard Temple
Los Angeles, California

Let's begin with an admission. Hard to acknowledge, especially publicly, but necessary. Usually I am pleased with invitations to tackle a subject, put down my thoughts, risk my opinions in written form. Flattery will buy my efforts and my essays.

So why have I nearly allowed the deadline for this essay to elapse? Why did I concoct almost every excuse possible to avoid writing down how I deal with the issues of non-Jews at Jewish celebrations? I certainly have constructed them, carefully I hope, over the course of years. Why, then, my reluctance to reveal them before the world?

I raise the question not to psychoanalyze my motives in public, but to expose the sensitivity so many of us have when dealing with non-Jews whom we encounter "dwelling in our midst," enriching our congregations with their spouses, their children, and often with their donations, money for dues and enthusiasms. We want them to "feel at home," not as strangers or aliens in our midst. We prefer to put our arms around them, and say, "It's great to have you here in our synagogue, wonderful to see how you support the Jewish loyalties of your loved ones. Thanks for being so accommodating, understanding, helpful and loving."

But -- ah, the awful "but."

Shall we go the next step? Treat the non-Jew as a Jew? Shall we allow our ritual to become playtime, make-believe-time, by inviting non-Jews to recite blessings in which the "us" is transformed into "them," and the meaning is demolished or corrupted in the extreme? What is the most civil, loving way in which to treat non-Jews at our Jewish celebrations?

The question is a tough one. It demands sensitivity, understanding, respect...fill in the rest, you know all of the words. Perhaps that is why I nearly failed to write this piece. I prefer to deal with each situation as unique -- even though I bring my set of guidelines and apply them. The point is that I am not dealing with hypothetical human beings when I meet with an intermarried couple about to celebrate their child's birth, bar/bat Mitzvah, or marriage. I am engaging with histories, sensibilities, and loyalties which are distinctive. Because they are, the human beings bearing them must be heard with caring, and counseled with reverence.

So much reverence that I must protect them from acting dishonestly, or appearing as counterfeits, that is to say from seeming to be what they are not. Non-Jews at a Jewish celebration are non-Jews sharing the celebration with Jews. Integrity demands that identities be sustained not abandoned, acknowledged and uplifted, not trivialized with forms of mimicry and masquerade.

Specifically, what does that mean when it comes to a non-Jewish parent at his/her child's Bar/Bat Mitzvah? Should s/he be invited to sit on the <u>bimah</u>, called upon for an <u>aliyah</u> in which s/he recites the words "who has chosen us from all peoples by giving us the Torah"? Should s/he be encouraged to address his/her child after the reading of Torah? Shall s/he be relegated to the status of observer with no part, no voice, no hug or kiss in this sacred, highly emotional ceremony of adolescence -- this historic bonding rite of his/her child to the Jewish people and tradition?

My practice is to promote the involvement of the non-Jewish parent in his/her child's Bar/Bat Mitzvah if that parent displays any inclination for such participation. "Sit on the pulpit with your child, walk with him/her to the Ark, stand with him/her while s/he reads from Torah, puff up with pride at his/her accomplishment, speak to him/her words of joy, respect and love for his/her study of his/her tradition, tell your child to be a loyal and responsible Jew."

I've said those words, or various renditions of them depending upon the parent, many times. The response has nearly always been relief. "Thanks," one father put it a few years ago, "you've allowed me to be myself and celebrate with my son."

By contrast what the parent had <u>not</u> been asked to do emphasizes what he had been free to do. We did not, to use the words of Rabbi Solomon B. Freehof's responsum, "require him to pronounce words which he does not believe and thus make of the blessing an insincere formality...." We did not ask him to pretend for just a day or an hour that he was a Jew, and to say "who has given us a Torah of truth." Instead, we made it possible for him to be a non-Jew at his son's Bar Mitzvah, and to be himself with his integrity preserved.

Can the same rule be applied to Shabbat and Festival celebrations in the home or synagogue, to life-cycle events, to other community occasions? I believe that it can and that it should. If truth is the seal of Torah, then it ought to be our highest aspiration. Masquerading in the synagogue is only allowed on Purim. Embracing non-Jews who celebrate our rites and rituals with us can be done with warmth and affection, and without forcing them to be what they are not and trivializing Jewish tradition.

Is it an accident that in Solomon B. Freehof's volume, <u>Current Responsa</u>, the responsum on the non-Jewish father's involvement at a Bar Mitzvah ceremony is followed by an article titled, "Halloween Masks"? Of course it is! No one would make the connection between the masks of one and the danger of mockery in the other. No one would do that - or would they? And even if Freehof never intended it, shouldn't we? Of course we should. That is we should if we want our non-Jewish loved ones to celebrate with us and afterwards to be able to look in the mirror and find themselves and not some mask of fakery and deception. We owe their support and love at least that, and we owe ourselves as much as well.

DISCUSSION QUESTIONS

1. How do non-Jews "enrich our congregations"? Is the author's suggestion that non-Jews enrich us shared by most members of your congregation?

2. Do you agree with Rabbi Fields' statement that to allow non-Jews to participate fully in Jewish rituals and ceremonies is to "treat the non-Jew as a Jew"? Why/why not?

3. The author notes that in dealing with intermarried couples, he is "engaging histories, sensitivities, and loyalties which are distinctive." What are the loyalties to which he refers?

4. In your experience, what do Jewish spouses want for their non-Jewish partners in relation to participation in the ceremonies the author describes? Do you think that this is generally the same as or different from what the non-Jewish partner would like?

5. The author comments that he is protecting non-Jews "from acting dishonestly or appearing as counterfeits" when he determines the nature of their involvement in Jewish rituals and ceremonies. Do non-Jews need to be protected in this way?

    How might they be acting dishonestly or appearing as counterfeits if they participated in particular rituals and ceremonies? What is a rabbi's role in this regard? What do the long-term best interests of Judaism dictate?

6. How can the separate identities of intermarried partners be sustained during life-cycle ceremonies in the synagogue?

7. Compare Rabbi Fields' perspective with that of Rabbi Hoffman. What is your reaction to their points of view?

****

Harvey J. Fields is a writer and Senior Rabbi of Wilshire Boulevard Temple, Los Angeles, California. His A Torah Commentary for Our Times, (Volume 1) was published in the summer of 1990 by UAHC Press.

The Role of the Non-Jewish Parent in Synagogue Life-Cycle Ceremonies: A Rabbi's Reflection

by
Rabbi Lawrence Mahrer
Congregation Beth Israel
Florence, South Carolina

As the number of intermarried families grows within the membership of all of our congregations, the issue of how non-Jews will participate in life-cycle ceremonies becomes increasingly important. It is no secret that it is often the inspiration derived from meaningful life-cycle ceremonies that serves as a catalyst to greater Jewish involvement. In our congregation, the ceremonies of Consecration and Bar/Bat Mitzvah strive to be inclusive of non-Jewish family members, without compromising the liturgy, theology and practice of Reform Judaism.

In the ceremony of Consecration, each child receives a gift of a miniature Torah scroll from our synagogue. While the ceremony itself focuses on the children, the commitment of Consecration is the parents', and they are included in the ceremony. Since children cannot fully understand the importance of the event and will not assume the responsibility of driving themselves to religious school each week, we are, in reality, consecrating a family to the religious education of the child.

If the child of an intermarried family is enrolled in our program of religious education, the non-Jewish parent must, minimally, consent to provide the child with a Jewish education; hopefully, there will be active support and some level of family involvement as well. Thus, after my introductory remarks to the Consecration ceremony, I ask both parents (if I am dealing with a two-parent family) to bring the child to the Ark. One parent takes the child's small Torah from the Ark, passes it to the other parent, who, in turn, gives it to the child. This participation symbolizes the support and the cooperation of the parent in the transmission of Torah and religious education of the child.

I have never had the experience of a non-Jewish parent refusing to participate at this level or expressing any discomfort. Many have said that they appreciated being included.

The ceremonies of Bar/Bat Mitzvah present some difficulties. In our Reform responsa literature, Freehof and Jacob[1] have taken

---

[1] The specific references to the Reform responsa literature are: <u>Modern Reform Responsa</u>, Solomon Freehof, HUC Press: 1971, p.69.; <u>American Reform Responsa</u>, Walter Jacob, Ed., CCAR: 1983, p.21.; <u>Contemporary Reform Responsa</u>, Walter Jacob, Ed., CCAR: 1987, pp. 240, 247.

similar positions on the involvement of a non-Jew in congregational worship. Generally speaking, both underscore that particularistic language which refers specifically to Jews should not be recited by non-Jews. Both use the Torah blessings as examples:

<u>Asher bachar banu</u>:....who has chosen us
<u>V'natan lanu</u>: .....and who has given us

Wording of this nature is inappropriate for non-Jews since they cannot be included among the "us".

While the language of certain portions of our liturgy may be particularistic to Jews, the importance of involving the non-Jewish parent in this significant life-cycle event cannot be dismissed. This has led to a number of suggestions designed to include the non-Jewish parent. In those congregations where the parents of B'nai Mitzvah lead the rituals of lighting Shabbat candles and reciting Kiddush at the beginning of Friday evening services, the wording included in <u>Gates of Prayer</u> might be changed slightly for the occasion. For example, the text of the candle lighting ritual from Service #1 in <u>Gates of Prayer</u> (p. 117) reads:

> Source of mercy, continue Your loving care for us and our loved ones. Give us strength to walk in Your presence on the paths of the righteous, loyal to Your Torah, steadfast in goodness.
>
> Keep far from us all shame, grief, and anguish; fill our homes with peace, light, and joy. O God, fountain of life, by Your light do we see light.
>
> Blessed is the Lord our God, Ruler of the universe, who hallows us with His Mitzvot, and commands us to kindle the lights of Shabbat.
>
> May God bless us with Shabbat joy.
> May God bless us with Shabbat holiness.
> May God bless us with Shabbat peace.

Simply by changing the word <u>TORAH</u> in line 3 to <u>TEACHING</u>, the text can be made suitable for a non-Jewish mother to recite on the occasion of the Bar/Bat Mitzvah of her child. It is assumed that this mother would read only the two top paragraphs, and while she is lighting the candles, the blessing would be sung in Hebrew by the congregation, the cantor/soloist or choir. The congregation would then respond with the bottom three lines. The non-Jewish mother would <u>not</u> read the English translation of the candle blessing.

In a similar fashion, the wording of the other seven candle lighting rituals could be modified to make them acceptable for recitation by a non-Jewish mother. Some are quite suitable as they are currently printed.

In a like manner, if the non-Jewish parent is the father, the words used to introduce the Kiddush in Gates of Prayer, (p. 719) can be modified to some extent. The original text is as follows:

> The seventh day is consecrated to the Lord our God. With wine, our symbol of joy, we celebrate this day and its holiness. We give thanks for all our blessings, for life and health, for work and rest, for home and love and friendship. On Shabbat, eternal sign of creation, we remember that we are created in the divine image. We therefore raise the cup in thanksgiving:
>
> Blessed is the Lord our God, Ruler of the universe, Creator of the fruit of the vine.
>
> Blessed is the Lord our God, Ruler of the universe, who hallows us with His Mitzvot and takes delight in us. In His love and favor He has made His holy Sabbath our heritage, as a reminder of the work of creation. It is first among our sacred days, and a remembrance of the Exodus from Egypt.
>
> O God, You have chosen us and set us apart from all the peoples, and in love and favor have given us the Sabbath day as a sacred inheritance. Blessed is the Lord, for the Sabbath and its holiness.

In efforts to include the non-Jewish father in this ritual, some have suggested that the wording might be changed along these lines:

> The seventh day is consecrated to the Lord. This day is celebrated and sanctified with wine, the Jewish symbol of joy. Our family gives thanks for all our blessings, for life and health, for work and rest, for home and love and friendship. On Shabbat, eternal sign of creation, we remember that we are created in the divine image. The kiddush cup is raised in thanksgiving.

At this point, the Hebrew of the Kiddush would be sung and the translation of the Kiddush would be omitted or read by the entire congregation, led by the rabbi.

For those congregations still using The Union Prayerbook, the solution is very much the same. The text of the candle lighting ritual (p. 7) appears below:

> Come, let us welcome the Sabbath. May its radiance illumine our hearts as we kindle these tapers.
>
> Light is the symbol of the divine. The Lord is my light and my salvation.

> Light is the symbol of the divine in man. The spirit of man is the light of the Lord.
>
> Light is the symbol of the divine law. For the commandment is a lamp and the law is a light.
>
> Light is the symbol of Israel's mission. I, the Lord, have set thee for a covenant of the people, for a light unto the nations.
>
> Therefore, in the spirit of our ancient tradition that hallows and unites Israel in all lands and all ages, do we now kindle the Sabbath lights.
>
> Blessed art Thou, O Lord our God, King of the universe, who hast sanctified us by Thy laws and commanded us to kindle the Sabbath light.
>
> May the Lord bless us with Sabbath joy.
> May the Lord bless us with Sabbath holiness.
> May the Lord bless us with Sabbath peace.

The final sentence before the Hebrew blessing could be rewritten:

> Therefore, in the spirit of the ancient tradition that hallows and unites people in all lands and all ages, do we now kindle the Sabbath lights.

And, again, as the candles are lit, the blessing is sung in Hebrew by the congregation, choir and/or cantor/soloist.

The wording of The Union Prayerbook Kiddush ritual (p. 93) is printed as follows:

> Let us praise God with this symbol of joy, and thank Him for the blessings of the past week, for life and strength, for home and love and friendship, for the discipline of our trials and temptations, for the happiness that has come to us out of our labors. Thou hast ennobled us, O God, by the blessings of work, and in love hast sanctified us by Sabbath rest and worship as ordained in the Torah: Six days shalt thou labor and do all thy work, but the seventh day is the Sabbath to be hallowed unto the Lord, thy God.
>
> Praised be Thou, O Lord our God, King of the universe, who hast created the fruit of the vine.

By changing the word TORAH to the FIVE BOOKS OF MOSES it becomes possible for a non-Jewish parent to read this for a congregation on the occasion of his child's Bar/Bat Mitzvah.

Non-Jewish parents may be included in the ceremony of passing the Torah from generation to generation, a particularly moving moment that I use at all B'nai Mitzvah in our congregation. The non-

Jewish grandparents do not participate in this ceremony. The non-Jewish parent is invited to stand with the Jewish parent before the open Ark. It is in part the consent, support and encouragement of the non-Jewish parent that has made the passing of Torah to the next generation possible. The actual passing of the Torah is from the Jewish parent to the child. When a non-Jewish parent is involved, I only give the Torah to one representative of each generation present, and only to the Jew in the parental generation. Care must be taken in the choice of words spoken as the Torah is moved from one generation to the next so as not to embarrass the non-Jewish parent by inclusion or exclusion. My own preference is to use something like this:

> In a few moments, (child's name), the scroll of Torah will be handed to you. But, first, we give it to one of your grandparents. The teachings of our religious heritage have come down to us through hundreds of generations. The strength and courage and dedication (Torah moved to parental generation) of all of those unknown and unnamed people have made it possible for us to stand before this Ark and this congregation on this important day (Torah passed to child) in your life. Now the Torah is yours. Hold it tightly. Guard it well. Carry it around this Sanctuary and through your life with pride, pleasure, happiness and blessing.

Finally, I offer each child the option of having his/her parents stand at the lectern while the Torah is read. Some B'nai Mitzvah are comfortable having their parents stand with them while they read from the Torah. Others prefer to have their parents seated in the congregation. The choice belongs to the child. Non-Jewish parents are included, at the child's request. Parents never recite the _Aliyah_ blessings; the child does. Non-Jewish parents have expressed gratitude for having been given the opportunity to stand publicly with their child while the Torah is read. It is a thrilling moment for everyone.

A final word of caution: intermarried families frequently approach public ritual ceremonies with uncertainty and some trepidation. This is especially true with regard to the B'nai Mitzvah ceremony, possibly because of all of the invited guests. Parents may be wary of the response of the rabbi to dealing with non-Jews in this forum and concerned that their child's experience will be affected by the presence and/or participation of non-Jewish family members. In a formal meeting between the rabbi and the parents, these concerns must be discussed privately and completely so that confusion and any feelings of inadequacy can be addressed.

The ceremonies of Consecration and Bar/Bat Mitzvah provide an opportunity for both the rabbi and the congregation to be welcoming and to offer support to intermarried couples who have made the commitment to raising their children as Jews.

Selections from <u>The Union Prayerbook</u> and <u>Gates of Prayer</u> copyright by the Central Conference of American Rabbis and used by permission.

DISCUSSION QUESTIONS:

1. The author states that the issue at hand is <u>how</u> intermarried families will participate in life-cycle ceremonies, not <u>whether</u> they should be included. Do you agree with the author's premise? Why/why not?

2. Many Reform Jews may agree in the abstract with the need to include non-Jewish family members, but find that the experience of such inclusion is problematic. What is your reaction to Rabbi Mahrer's description of the way Consecration ceremonies are held at his congregation? What aspects do you like? Dislike? How would Rabbi Mahrer's suggestions work in your congregation?

3. In contrast to Temple Beth Israel's practice, many congregations <u>do</u> customarily honor B'nai Mitzvah parents with an <u>aliyah</u> or <u>aliyot</u>. Rabbi Jeffrey Salkin (Central Synagogue of Nassau County, Rockville Centre, NY) has created a blessing in English that may be read by the non-Jewish parent after the Jewish parent has recited the Torah blessing in Hebrew:

    > O God of all humanity:
    >
    > We lift our voices in gratitude that the Torah has come into the world through the Jewish people.
    >
    > We lift our voices in gratitude that our son today takes his place among the people of Israel. We pray that he will do so with pride and joy. As you called Israel to be a light to the nations, so, too, we pray that our son will be his own ray of light to the world.

    Is there a difference between inserting a new prayer and rewording a prayer or blessing from the familiar, printed liturgy? Do you feel more comfortable with one than the other? Why/why not?

4. What is a rabbi's responsibility to intermarried families? To the congregation as a whole? To Reform Judaism's collective future?

5. Whose decision is the adaptation of ritual for intermarried families? The rabbi's? The ritual committee's? The intermarried family's? Does anyone have ultimate authority in this regard?

6. What implications will the inclusion of non-Jews in rituals previously performed exclusively by Jews have for the welfare of our congregations? For the future of the Reform movement?

7. Are there implications for <u>K'lal Yisrael</u> and for our

relationship with other branches of Judaism when we adapt ritual in the manner the author suggests? Is this an appropriate area for concern?

8. Rabbi Mahrer notes that many intermarried families approach life cycle ceremonies with uncertainty and trepidation. What is the cause of this uncertainty? What can be done in your congregation to make families more comfortable at such important points in their lives?

9. What implications does Rabbi Mahrer's article have for the way membership is handled in Reform congregations? Should intermarried families be solicited for membership and told that there are ways in which non-Jewish family members can be included in worship and life-cycle ritual? What is important for prospective members in general to understand about the congregation's policies in this regard?

10. Are there some ritual acts that should be reserved for Jews only? If so, what involvement in ritual is inappropriate for non-Jews and on what basis are the parameters established?

11. What will the impact be on worshippers as a whole if non-Jews are on the bimah, participating in public ritual? What are the positive aspects? What are the negative aspects?

12. Are children's services different from adult services with regard to the participation of non-Jews?

13. Do non-Jews sing in your choir? Provide High Holy Day music? What are the implications of this involvement?

14. What is the current custom in your congregation regarding participation of non-Jews?

15. Are B'nai Mitzvah, where involvement of all family members may be the norm, different from regular Sabbath services? Why/why not?

16. What is the congregation's obligation in promoting ritual continuity as opposed to responding to individual needs?

The Role of the Non-Jew and the Temple Constitution

by
Rabbi Sally J. Priesand
Monmouth Reform Temple
Tinton Falls, New Jersey

One day I was standing in the hall speaking to our Religious School principal, when a teacher came out of her classroom and said: "Rabbi, my class would like to know if non-Jews can be counted in the minyan" Realizing that the majority of students in this particular class had one non-Jewish parent, I hesitated and then replied: "In our synagogue, the answer is yes." The principal told me that he thought I had made a mistake and that I should have said no. As I walked back to my study, I realized that this was but one of many incidents that were becoming commonplace in our congregation, and that all too often, in an attempt to be sensitive to the increasing number of non-Jews among us, we were beginning to misrepresent Judaism. That was the day I decided to ask our Constitution Committee to consider the role of non-Jews in Temple life and to adopt a policy that would protect and preserve the Jewishness of our congregation.

Changing our constitution with regard to this issue was a long and painful process. Nonetheless, it gave our members an opportunity to grapple with an important question of philosophy; to discuss with each other who we are and where we are going; to establish a clear-cut policy that could be presented openly and honestly to prospective members; and to resolve this matter before a problem arose with a specific individual. All in all, it was an opportunity for growth, and our congregation is stronger for having participated in the process, which I am about to describe for you in detail.

In January of 1988, a committee was appointed to review our constitution. Although the role of non-Jews in our congregation was only one of many issues it was asked to consider, every effort was made to appoint a committee of people with a wide range of differing views, including some members whose spouses were not Jewish. In order to make certain all issues would be discussed, we began by considering the following statement based on suggestions by the UAHC in the "Model Constitution":

> "Non-Jewish partners are welcome to share in the fellowship of the congregation and are encouraged to participate in its activities. However, the privileges of voting, of serving on the Board, holding office, chairing a committee and participating in certain ritual practices as agreed upon by the Rabbi and Ritual Committee shall be reserved to Jews-by-Birth and Jews-by-Choice."

Because we felt strongly that our decision should be an informed one, based on knowledge and not emotion, we read and studied together a collection of responsa relating to non-Jewish participation in Temple activities. (See <u>Contemporary American Reform Responsa</u>, Walter Jacob, CCAR: 1987, pp. 240-248.)

In the course of our discussion, two issues began to surface:

1) how best to keep a record of who is Jewish and who is not. (We discovered, for example, that a non-Jewish spouse, who considered herself a member of the Temple and had participated on the <u>bimah</u>, was also active in a local church.)

2) what should be the role of non-Jews on the <u>bimah</u> and in leadership positions. (The Ritual Committee was finding it increasingly difficult to know who to invite for <u>aliyot</u>, and some committee chairs had expressed discomfort in deciding who should serve on their committees).

After several meetings and countless hours of thoughtful discussion, the Constitution Committee drafted amendments that it deemed appropriate for our Temple and presented them to the Board in March. Two members of the congregation, both involved in mixed marriages and opposed to the amendments, also presented their views. After much discussion, the Board approved the committee's recommendations, which were then mailed to the congregation in preparation for the annual meeting. Included in the proposed amendments were the following policies:

* that non-Jews seeking to be permanently identified with Judaism and not actively participating in another religion be welcomed as members of our Temple;

* that a record be kept indicating who is Jewish and who is not; and

* that a distinction be made between the privileges of membership for all members and those for Jewish members.

At the Annual Meeting in April, all members of the congregation, both Jewish and non-Jewish, had an opportunity to discuss the proposed amendments and vote on them. The discussion was often heated; tempers flared, and opinions were expressed with vehemence, indignation and passion. Some people felt that the proposed amendments were discriminatory and that we were establishing two classes of membership. The analogy of citizenship in a country was unacceptable to them, and they were offended by the suggestion that a record would be kept indicating who was Jewish and who was not.

Some thought that because they were raising their children as Jews, they had the right to participate in every aspect of Temple life. Others held the opposite view, reminding those present that a synagogue is not a social club, but an institution charged with ensuring the Jewish future, and that non-Jews should not be involved in policy-making, especially with regard to matters of ritual and religious education. Several Jews-by-Choice presented moving statements, both eloquent and emotional, expressing their belief that those who had not made a total commitment to Judaism should not be entitled to all the privileges. Members of our Senior Youth Group touched our hearts with their impassioned plea to preserve Jewish tradition. Because we were four families short of a quorum, no final decision could be made at the meeting. It was a painful experience (matters of growth and change often are), and most everyone left feeling hurt and unsettled.

A sub-committee of the Board was appointed to review and revise the proposed amendments in light of the comments and suggestions made at the annual meeting. The result of this effort was mailed to the congregation in preparation for a special meeting, called for the sole purpose of considering constitutional amendments. This time the Board was particularly sensitive to the format in which the amendments were presented. Everything was simplified as much as possible. Each page of the packet contained three headings:

1) "Current constitution reads"

2) "Proposed change"

3) "Reason for change"

The committee had also attempted to write the proposed amendments in a more positive way, emphasizing the relationship between privileges of membership and the traditional functions of a synagogue as House of Study, House of Prayer and House of Assembly. In addition, it was recommended that the record indicating who is Jewish and who is not would be kept only by the rabbi.

Every effort was made to ensure that all members of the congregation were aware of the discussion that would take place at the special meeting. Members of the Board called every Temple family, encouraging them to come to the meeting and participate in the decision-making process. Moreover, the rabbi called several families involved in mixed marriages who had expressed strong opposition to the proposed amendments and offered to meet with them individually. Some accepted the invitation; others did not.

It is also important to note that over the years our congregation has been deeply involved in issues of Outreach. We have an active Outreach Committee which has worked diligently to make our congregation warm and welcoming. As a result, nearly one-third of our membership consists of families in which one spouse is not Jewish. During the period when constitutional changes were being discussed, the Outreach Committee continued to function and to sponsor a variety of programs which included our annual Outreach Shabbat on which Mel Merians, Chairman of the UAHC-CCAR Commission on Reform Jewish Outreach, was invited to address the congregation. Although the service was well-attended, most of those opposed to the constitutional changes did not attend.

The special congregational meeting was held in June. Once again, the discussion was heated. Temple leaders were accused of being narrow-minded and spreading hatred. Some people thought this was the first step of a hidden agenda, when in fact it was an attempt on our part to be more sensitive to the needs of all our members, and at the same time, to ensure the continued Jewishness of our congregation. Several people walked out in protest when the following amendments passed by a two-thirds vote:

- A. Temple Membership
  Article II - Membership
  Section I - Members

  Upon approval by the Board of Trustees, any person of the Jewish faith or any person seeking to be permanently identified with Judaism and not actively participating in another religion is a member of the Congregation of Monmouth Reform Temple. The rabbi shall keep a record indicating who is Jewish and who is not. A child of any member is also a member, provided that the child is not practicing another religion. Any child who is a member and who either marries or attains age 21 and is self-supporting shall no longer be considered a member of the Congregation until such child has applied and been accepted for membership.

- B. Privileges of Membership
  Article III - Privileges of Membership

  A non-delinquent member of the Congregation shall be entitled to privileges of membership, subject to the rules, regulations and fees prescribed by the Board of Trustees.

  <u>Section 1</u>: These privileges shall include:

  - a. The right to enjoy the fellowship of the Congregation.
  - b. The right to receive education in the Jewish tradition.
  - c. The right to be seated in the House of Worship of the Congregation at all times including the High Holy Days.

        d.   The right to participate in ritual practices, the specifics of which will be determined by the Ritual Committee and rabbi.

        e.   The right to vote at all meetings of the Congregation, if either Confirmed or over the age of 18.

        f.   The right to use the Temple building for approved functions.

Section 2: The following privileges require membership in the Jewish faith, through either birth or conversion:

        a.   The right to receive religious education in preparation for Bar/Bat Mitzvah and/or Confirmation, and to receive same in the House of Worship of the Congregation.

        b.   The right to be elected as an officer or trustee of the Congregation.

        c.   The right to chair a Standing Committee.

        d.   The right to be elected as president of an Auxiliary of the Congregation.

        e.   The right to be appointed to the following Standing Committees: Israel, Jewish Philanthropy, Religious Education, Ritual, UAHC.

These amendments are now part of our Temple Constitution, but not without consequence. Four families resigned their membership, and a handful of others decided to curtail their involvement in Temple activities.

In hindsight, we could have eliminated any constitutional reference to the keeping of a record and merely asked for the information, as we do now, on our application form. Furthermore, we could have emphasized more than we did all the positive things our Temple has to offer the non-Jewish spouse. And finally we could have organized small group discussions in people's homes in which those involved in mixed marriages who agreed with the changes (and there were many) could discuss the issues with those who disagreed. Perhaps in an informal setting we could have lessened some of the hurt, fear and anger. This may also have given us the opportunity to deal with other underlying issues that were obviously bothering some of our mixed married families. I suspect, however, that none of the above actions would have made any real difference because the issue is just too sensitive ever to be simple.

As I write these words, a year and a half has passed since we changed our constitution. For the most part, the issue has been laid to rest, and those who had previously curtailed their involvement are beginning to participate again. Those who thought we had a hidden agenda have realized that we did not. We simply wanted to have a policy that we could turn to should the occasion arise. Our only regret is that we did not establish the policy several years sooner. If we had, perhaps we would not have lost any families over this issue because when they joined they would have understood clearly and unequivocally the role of non-Jews in the life of our Temple. We are grateful that the matter was resolved before a problem arose with a specific individual, and we encourage every congregation to consider constitutional changes as soon as possible. The longer you wait the more difficult it will be.

DISCUSSION QUESTIONS:

1. What is your reaction, as a temple leader, to Rabbi Priesand's description of the process of constitutional change at her congregation? What did you like about how it was handled? What would you change?

2. What is your view of the rabbi's response to the religious school teacher regarding whether non-Jews can be counted in a <u>minyan</u>?

3. Rabbi Priesand begins by noting that "...in an attempt to be sensitive to the increasing numbers of non-Jews among us, we were beginning to misrepresent Judaism." What does she mean? Describe the "misrepresentation" she is referring to.

4. What does the author mean by "non-Jews seeking to be permanently identified with Judaism?"

5. Are lists of who is Jewish and who is not necessary? Why/why not? How can this information be obtained in the least offensive manner?

6. This congregation relied upon the advice in Jewish sources and guidelines provided by the UAHC in the "model constitution." Contrast this advice with Rabbi Hoffman's perspective as outlined in his article, "Non-Jews and Jewish Life-Cycle Liturgy."

7. What do constitutional changes such as those described by the author mean in terms of membership recruitment?

8. What do you know about the policies regarding non-Jews at other congregations in your area?

9. Should non-Jews be permitted to serve on committees? (PTA, school, building and grounds, finance, ritual, social action, etc.) Which committees might be appropriate? Inappropriate? Why/why not?

10. Should a non-Jew be eligible to chair a committee? Why/why not?

11. Should non-Jews be eligible for positions on the Sisterhood or Men's Club board?

12. Should non-Jews become members of the congregation's Board of Trustees? May they become congregational officers?

13. What decisions in the life of the congregation should be made only by Jews? (Choosing a rabbi? Adult education or religious school decisions? Decisions about ritual practice?)

14. While congregations may want to be warm and welcoming, where should they draw the line? Are policy decisions likely to be seen as rejections or challenges?

15. Who is a "non-Jew?" Someone who practices another faith? Someone who practices no faith? Someone who is "all but converted?"

16. Will allowing non-Jews to become members encourage or discourage conversion?

17. How will the "culture" of your congregation be affected by potential numbers of non-Jews who are members? What might be the positive and negative influences of non-Jewish members?

18. Will permitting non-Jews to become members encourage intermarriage? What "message" will your policy convey, especially to the congregation's youth? What are the potential positive messages? Negative messages?

19. Does the proposed wording of your constitution reflect differences in considering non-Jewish <u>individuals</u> as well as non-Jews who are part of an intermarried family?

20. In your setting, would you prefer an "open forum" approach to constitutional change, or would the Board make and implement decisions without a public process? Should non-Jews have input during the process?

21. When decisions are made about changing <u>your</u> constitution, how will you communicate policy to the congregation? Will the process be similar to that described by Rabbi Priesand? Whose responsibility is it to communicate policy?

SECTION FOUR

APPLYING WHAT WE HAVE LEARNED

Making Congregational Policy

After grappling with the issues described in this resource and considering the particular needs of your congregation, the time comes to translate your discussions into temple policy. This section will provide an overview of considerations for incorporating your decisions into your congregation's constitution.

Membership

In considering the role of non-Jews in congregational life, the central issue often is the polarity between the desire to bring non-Jews close to the community, to encourage them to convert or raise their children as Jews, and the need to maintain the integrity of Judaism and Jewish practice. How can the congregation strike a balance between these two poles?

The vast majority of UAHC congregations allows non-Jews to be members with certain restrictions. In general, the unit of membership is not the individual, but the family. The non-Jew may be a member within the context of a family membership. The following are examples of how some congregations have handled the membership issue in their constitution:

> In the case of married persons the unit of membership shall be the family. For the purpose of this article the family shall be construed to mean husband, wife, and their unmarried children who are not self-supporting and/or residing in another community while attending an educational institution. A non-Jewish spouse shall be considered a member in good standing and welcome to share in the fellowship of the Congregation. Voting privileges and the holding of office in all facets of congregational life, the Board of Trustees, committees and Congregational meetings shall be reserved to Jews-by-Birth and Jews-by-Choice.
> (Excerpted from the UAHC Model Constitution)

Another perspective on membership comes from the following constitution, which considers the unit of membership to be either the individual or the family:

> Any person of the Jewish faith by birth or by choice, according to Reform Jewish rabbinic criteria, may be elected to membership in the Congregation on approval of his/her application by the Board of Trustees...

> ...The unit of membership shall be the individual, or in the case of married persons, the family. In the case of a family membership, the husband and wife shall each have one vote where the member is entitled to vote. In addition, each child of a member family who has attained the age of sixteen (16) years and who applies for membership in the Congregation shall likewise be entitled to vote so long as the member family is entitled to vote and such child is unmarried and permanently residing in the family home. Non-Jewish spouses and non-

> Jewish children shall be considered members of the Congregational family.

In order to solve the problem of knowing who is Jewish and who is not within congregational membership, one congregation described membership this way in their constitution:

> Upon approval by the Board of Trustees, any person of the Jewish faith or any person seeking to be permanently identified with Judaism and not actively participating in another religion is a member of the Congregation.... The rabbi shall keep a record indicating who is Jewish and who is not. A child of any member is also a member, provided that the child is not practicing another religion. Any child who is a member and who either marries or attains age 21 and is self-supporting shall no longer be considered a member of the Congregation until such child has applied and been accepted for membership.

Note that this congregation will accept as a member anyone "seeking to be permanently identified with Judaism and not actively participating in another religion...." This may include a single person who has begun the journey toward conversion. (See Appendix I for examples of Congregational Membership Application Forms which seek to identify in a sensitive manner who is Jewish and who is not.)

Leadership

While the issue of membership may be relatively easily addressed, deciding whether or not some privileges of membership ought to be reserved solely for Jews often becomes a more difficult issue. In considering who may be elected or appointed to office at any level in the congregation, it is important to remember that temple leaders have a dual responsibility: to make decisions for the current, day-to-day operations of the congregation, and to shape the broader future of the temple and, by extension, of Reform Judaism as well.

In most UAHC congregations, non-Jews who are members do not hold office. Constitutions address this matter in different ways. One congregation chose to describe the general rights and privileges of membership, and to address the role of non-Jews separately:

> A member in good standing shall, except as otherwise limited in the CONSTITUTION or these BY-LAWS, have the following rights, privileges, and benefits:
>
> A. The right to vote at all meetings of the Congregation.
>
> B. The right of admittance at all religious services for himself and his family.
>
> C. The right to participate in all activities of the Congregation and to join its affiliated bodies.

- D. The right to stand for election and to hold office as an officer or trustee.

- E. The right to have his children receive a religious education in the Religious School of the Congregation and to be prepared for Bar or Bat Mitzvah and Confirmation and, upon qualifying, to receive the same in the Temple.

Non-Jewish spouses ...shall be considered members of the Congregational family. They shall have all rights enunciated in Section 7 of the by-laws except the rights to vote at meetings of the Congregation, to hold committee or sub-committee chairs, or to hold office as an officer or trustee.

Another congregation amended its constitution. The writers note:

There has been much discussion about the sensitive nature of membership and its privileges. In an effort to recognize and accommodate the needs of all our members, while assuring the continued Jewishness of our congregation, the Board has proposed (and subsequently adopted) the following:

A non-delinquent member of the Congregation shall be entitled to privileges of membership, subject to the rules, regulations and fees prescribed by the Board of Trustees.

These privileges shall include:

- A. The right to enjoy the fellowship of the Congregation.

- B. The right to receive education in the Jewish tradition.

- C. The right to be seated in the House of Worship of the Congregation at all times including the High Holy Days.

- D. The right to participate in ritual practices, the specifics of which will be determined by the Ritual Committee and rabbi.

- E. The right to vote at all meetings of the Congregation, if either Confirmed or over the age of 18.

- F. The right to use the Temple building for approved functions.

The following privileges require membership in the Jewish faith, through either birth or conversion:

A. The right to receive religious education in preparation for Bar/Bat itzvah and/or Confirmation, and to receive same in the House of Worship of the Congregation.

B. The right to be elected as an officer or trustee of the Congregation.

C. The right to chair a Standing Committee.

D. The right to be elected as president of an Auxiliary of the Congregation.

E. The right to be appointed to the following Standing Committees: Israel, Jewish Philanthropy, Religious Education, Ritual, UAHC.

Ritual

The third area to be clarified is the role of the non-Jew in ritual. Jewish law distinguishes between public and private ritual. Public ritual acts include the following: aliyah; Shabbat candles, Kiddush, and Motzi in the context of a worship service; passing the Torah l'dor vador (from generation to generation); sitting on the bimah; opening the ark; reading prayers in English or in Hebrew; blessing a child, etc. Private ritual generally refers to ritual in the home or in private life-cycle events that are separate from congregational worship (and which are, therefore, generally exempt from governance by the congregation's constitution.) One congregation has prepared the following statement regarding the participation of non-Jews in public ritual:

> Non-Jews are warmly welcome to attend worship services and, upon invitation of the rabbis, participate in leading worship. The role they shall exercise in leading the worship, whether at regularly scheduled services or at life-cycle events, shall be determined by the Senior Rabbi. He/she shall use as a general guide Responsum #6 as it appears in American Reform Responsa (Walter Jacob, Ed., CCAR:1983) entitled, "Participation of Non-Jews in a Jewish Public Service," understanding that the Board recognizes that recommendation #3 ("through the recitation of prayers for special family occasions") be broadened to include all Congregational services.

It will be important to confer with your rabbi, Consititution Committee and Ritual Committee during your discussions, since they are responsible for decisions about worship. You will find discussion on the adaptation of ritual for the purpose of including non-Jews in the articles by Rabbi Harvey Fields, Rabbi Joseph Glaser, Rabbi Lawrence Hoffman, Rabbi W. Gunther Plaut and Rabbi Lawrence Mahrer. Rabbi Lester Bronstein's piece titled, "Exploring Jewish Prayer and Ritual," teaches about Jewish prayer and ritual and may be useful in helping the rabbi and appropriate committees establish a basis for decision-making regarding the involvement of non-Jews in ritual. "Guidelines from Our Sources: Selected Reform Responsa" contains selected responsa which may also be helpful.

APPENDICES

APPENDIX I

MEMBERSHIP AND RELIGIOUS BACKGROUND
Excerpts from Congregational Membership Forms

In order for the congregation to be effective in meeting the needs of the entire membership -- born Jews, Jews-by-Choice and intermarried families, it is important to know the makeup of the congregation and to ascertain what needs can be met through sensitivity training of leadership and staff, special Outreach programs and support groups. Rabbis, educators and administrators are often involved in the initial intake interview. The way in which this interview is handled sends an important message to potential members regarding the temple's receptivity to them.

Information on conversion is obtained for the purpose of reaching out to those new Jews who may not yet feel comfortable enough to join the congregation's adult education program, or who may have questions or want the support of special programs for new Jews. The ultimate goal of any such program is to assist Jews-by-Choice in becoming fully integrated into the Jewish community and the life of the congregation.

Temple policy regarding the involvement of non-Jewish spouses and family members ought to be made known to all congregants from the start in order to avoid any misunderstandings or embarrassment. It is also important that those in leadership positions and those on the Ritual Committee are aware of this information so that congregational policy can be upheld and individuals can be spared unnecessary embarrassment.

One way of ensuring the confidentiality of this information is for the rabbi to make it available on a need-to-know basis, using his or her discretion as to when this is most appropriate.

Circumstances do arise when the educator, and perhaps a teacher, should be made aware of certain information which could be helpful in reaching out more effectively to a child or family. Sometimes it is sufficient to let teachers know what percentage of students in their classes have a non-Jewish parent or non-Jewish relatives. Such information may affect the content and presentation of particular lessons and assignments. It may be helpful for the educator to know if the non-Jew is currently practicing another religion, as this sometimes affects the child's religious identity development. It is not uncommon for congregations to request this information on the religious school registration form.

The inclusion of questions regarding religious background serves to normalize the status of born Jews, Jews-by-Choice or intermarried couples. By asking these questions outright, and not simply allowing for a designation of "other," the application form tells the new member that s/he is not alone and that others in the congregation share a similar situation.

Any information obtained through the temple membership application should be used in a positive manner to create a warm, welcoming environment in the temple. Information on religious background is useful in helping the lay and professional leadership meet the needs of the congregation. Some rabbis acquire this information informally, through an interview process. Others use the congregational membership form as a source of information. Regardless of what method is employed by a particular congregation, it is important that the information be acquired and used appropriately and with discretion.

The following are excerpts from selected congregational membership forms on how information concerning religious background might be obtained.

APPENDIX I

MEMBERSHIP AND RELIGIOUS BACKGROUND:
Excerpts from Congregational Membership Forms

In order for the congregation to be effective in meeting the needs of the entire membership - born Jews, Jews-by-Choice and intermarried families, it is important to know the makeup of the congregation and to ascertain what needs can be met through sensitivity training of leadership and staff, special Outreach programs and support groups. Rabbis, educators and administrators are often involved in the inital intake interview. The way in which this interview is handled sends an important message to potential members regarding the temple's receptivity to them.

Information on conversion is obtained for the purpose of reaching out to those new Jews who may not yet feel comfortable enough to matriculate into the congregation's adult education program, or who may have questions or want the support of special programs for new Jews. The ultimate goal of any such program is to assist Jews-by-Choice in becoming fully integrated into the Jewish community and the life of the congregation.

Temple policy regarding the involvement of non-Jewish spouses and family members ought to be made known to all congregants from the start in order to avoid any misunderstandings or embarrassment. It is also important that those in leadership positions and those on the Ritual Committee are aware of this information so that congregational policy can be upheld and individuals can be spared unnecessary embarrassment.

One way of ensuring the confidentiality of this information is for the rabbi to make it available on a need-to-know basis, using his or her discretion as to when this is most appropriate.

Circumstances do arise when the educator, and perhaps a teacher, should be made aware of certain information which could be helpful in reaching out more effectively to a child or family. Sometimes it is sufficient to let teachers know what percentage of students in their classes have a non-Jewish parent or non-Jewish relatives. Such information may affect the content and presentation of particular lessons and assignments. It may be helpful for the educator to know if the non-Jew is currently practicing another religion, as this sometimes affects the child's religious identity development. It is not uncommon for congregations to request this information on the religious school registration form.

The inclusion of questions regarding religious background serves to normalize the status of born Jews, Jews-by-Choice or intermarried couples. By asking these questions outright, and not simply allowing for a designation of "other," the applicant is being made aware of the fact that s/he is not alone and that others in the congregation share a similar situation.

Any information obtained through the temple membership application should be used in a positive manner to create a warm, welcoming environment in the temple. Information on religious background is useful in helping the lay and professional leadership meet the needs of the congregation. Some rabbis acquire this information informally, through an interview process. Others use the congregational membership form as a source of information. Regardless of what method is employed by a particular congregation, it is important that the information be acquired and used appropriately and with discretion.

The following are excerpts from selected congregational membership forms on how information concerning religious background might be obtained.

TEMPLE JEREMIAH
937 Happ Road - P.O. Box 8209, Northfield, Illinois 60093 441-5760

APPLICATION FOR MEMBERSHIP

We (I) hereby apply for membership in Temple Jeremiah, a congregation dedicated to the principles of Reform Judaism. Our primary goals are the enhancement of our religious experience, the continuing education of our members and their children, and a commitment to humanity.

RELIGIOUS BACKGROUND

☐ Reform   ☐ Conservative   ☐ Orthodox   ☐ None

☐ Non Jewish (Religion Practiced) _____

☐ Convert to Judaism (year) _____

Date of Bat Mitzvah ____/____/____   Year of Confirmation _____

Previous Community and Congregational Affiliation _____

2 NORTH SHORE CONGREGATION ISRAEL
1185 Sheridan Road • Glencoe, Illinois 60022 • 312/835-0724

MEMBERSHIP FAMILY RECORD

12. Religious tradition in which you were raised (Check One)
If not raised in the Jewish tradition are you (Check One)

☐ Reform ☐ Conservative ☐ Orthodox ☐ Secular

☐ Jewish by choice ☐ Non-Jewish

Denomination: _____

Did your Jewish education include: (Check appropriate boxes)

☐ Bat Mitzvah Date _____ Confirmation Date _____

Congregation Name: _____

City: _____ State: _____

---

12. Religious tradition in which you were raised (Check One)
If not raised in the Jewish tradition are you (Check One)

☐ Reform ☐ Conservative ☐ Orthodox ☐ Secular

☐ Jewish by choice ☐ Non-Jewish

Denomination: _____

Did your Jewish education include: (Check appropriate boxes)

☐ Bar Mitzvah Date _____ Confirmation Date _____

Congregation Name: _____

City: _____ State: _____

3 TEMPLE HAR ZION
7360 Bayview Avenue • Thornhill, Ontario L3T 2R7 Canada

RELIGIOUS SCHOOL REGISTRATION FORM

Is any member of your immediate family who lives at home not Jewish? (This is important information for the rabbi)

4. THE CONGREGATION BETH ISRAEL
ORGANIZED 1843
701 FARMINGTON AVENUE, WEST HARTFORD, CT 06119 (201) 233-8215

Date _____

Name: Mr. / Mrs. / Miss. / _____

_____
Last   First (Both first names if couple)   Middle

Residence _____
Street   City & Zip Code   Home Telephone

Marital Status: Married _____ Single _____ Widowed _____ Divorced _____ Separated _____
Mo. Day Yr.

Are both husband and wife born Jews? Yes ☐ No ☐

Is either a convert to Judaism? Husband ☐ Wife ☐

Where converted? _____ When converted? _____

By whom? _____ Address _____

Is either not a Jew-by-birth and not formally converted? Husband ☐ _____ Wife ☐ _____

---

5. OLD YORK ROAD TEMPLE - BETH AM
971 Old York Road, Abington, Pennsylvania 19001

CENSUS FORM

ADULT MALE		Names of Professional Organizations (and positions held) of which you are a member	ADULT FEMALE	
☐ Jewish By Birth ☐ Jewish By Choice ☐ Not Jewish		What is your religious status?	☐ Jewish By Birth ☐ Jewish By Choice ☐ Not Jewish	
☐ Single (never married) ☐ Married ☐ Separated ☐ Divorced ☐ Widowed		Marital Status	☐ Single (never married) ☐ Married ☐ Separated ☐ Divorced ☐ Widowed	
___ / ___ / ___		Month/Day/Year of present marriage	___ / ___ / ___	
		Name of previous congregation		
		City & State of previous congregation		
☐ Reform ☐ Conservative ☐ Orthodox ☐ Other: ___		Type of Jewish Background	☐ Reform ☐ Conservative ☐ Orthodox ☐ Other: ___	
☐ Bar Mitzvah ☐ Jewish/Hebrew Day School ☐ Confirmation ☐ Post-Confirmation Religious Schooling		Please check all that apply to you:	☐ Bar Mitzvah ☐ Jewish/Hebrew Day School ☐ Confirmation ☐ Post-Confirmation Religious Schooling	

APPENDIX II

UAHC AFFILIATES: GUIDELINES REGARDING NON-JEWISH MEMBERS

NFTS Policy Guidelines Regarding Non-Jewish Sisterhood Members

The NFTS Constitution is predicated on the fact that local Sisterhood members are Jewish and the criteria for group affiliation is a membership of Jewish women. Therefore there is no special note or special conditions regarding non-Jews.

The Model Constitution developed for local Sisterhood use is based on this same premise. However, some 20 or more years ago the number of questions asked about non-Jewish members, paralleling questions asked about membership of Jewish women who were not temple members, resulted in rephrasing the Model Constitution to take these two situations into account.

"Open" membership was recommended for local Sisterhoods in given situations, no recommendation either favoring or excluding non-Jewish members was made, but in both situations language was included to put into place a constitutional requirement that in order to be elected to a leadership position a woman must both be a member of the congregation and Jewish. (A copy of the Model Constitution can be obtained from NFTS.)

Within the last two or three years some questions have been raised as to whether the NFTS Constitution itself should state explicitly that NFTS is an organization for Jewish women. Our leadership felt this change was unnecessary and, in fact, weakened the Constitution. They also did not feel the need to incorporate special reference to non-Jewish women. A Board recommendation was adopted, however, stating that when NFTS solicits from local Sisterhoods names of women to be considered for election to the NFTS Board of Directors, one of the criteria is that the women must be Jewish for election to the NFTS Board of Directors. It has long been a requirement that the congregation to which her Sisterhood was connected was a UAHC affiliate.

The 13 NFTS District Federations, as subsidiaries of NFTS, must follow the NFTS Constitution and its policies. Therefore a woman active in a NFTS District Federation leadership role must be Jewish and her Sisterhood must be a member of a UAHC-affiliated congregation. The only exception to either of these conditions is if the District Board includes ex-officio membership of every Sisterhood President (in addition to its elected Board member body and its leadership); this woman may serve on the Board but may not be elected or appointed to a leadership position.

The NFTS policy is not binding upon a local Sisterhood since the Sisterhood is "autonomous of NFTS," but it is not autonomous of its congregation. Therefore if there is misunderstanding, confusion or seeming violation of NFTS policy, it is because the congregational policy is not clear. If the congregation allows non-Jews to vote or be elected to a leadership role, the Sisterhood may also reflect this policy. But the local situation may not determine or alter NFTS requirements and those applicable to its District Federations.

The fundamental premise of the NFTS policies, both those that are legal by virtue of constitutional or Board action, and those that are recommended to a local Sisterhood, is that decision-making for a Jewish religious organization can only be made by those who are fully committed to that religious point of view. Nevertheless, NFTS recognizes that it is through the local Sisterhood that many non-Jewish spouses find an arena through which they can express a supportive role to the Jewish spouse, and to the children if they are being raised as Jews, as well as develop greater sensitivity and familiarity with Jewish customs, home observances and Jewish ritual while at the same time helping to enable the Sisterhood to fulfill its commitments and responsibilities to the synagogue and the community. Therefore NFTS has encouraged local Sisterhoods to extend a hand of friendship and encourage participation in Sisterhood always underscoring that participation is not the equivalent in its full sense.

Eleanor Schwartz,
Executive Director of National Federation of Temple Sisterhoods

NFTB Guidelines Regarding Non-Jewish Brotherhood Members

Brotherhood, as in the National Federation of Temple Brotherhoods, is a proper noun. But in practice, Brotherhood is an active verb, a way of living.

While the NFTB Constitution defines a Brotherhood as "any organization of ten or more men who believe in the principles of Judaism," the Constitution further states that members of a Brotherhood must be "affiliated with a Reform Jewish congregation" unless they reside in a "locality where there is no Reform Jewish congregation." (A copy of the Model Constitution can be obtained from NFTB.)

There are non-Jewish Brotherhood members who do not believe in the principles of Judaism (at least not actively) but do belong to a Reform congregation as the spouse of a Jewish woman. There are also a few cases where non-Jewish men have joined a local Brotherhood (but not a temple) due to their interest in the fellowship of Judaism.

In these cases, NFTB is pleased to have these men as members of our local clubs although they may not serve as president.

NFTB is, in fact, very open to the participation of non-Jews in Brotherhood activities because it provides an opportunity for people to work together in the common cause of striving to create a better world.

And this, ultimately, is the goal of Brotherhood.

Lewis Eisenberg,
Executive Director of National Federation of Temple Brotherhoods

APPENDIX III

OUTREACH-RELATED RESPONSA
from the Various Volumes of Solomon Freehof
and AMERICAN REFORM RESPONSA, CCAR, 1983

A. CONVERSION

Title	VOL.	ENTRY #	PAGE #
Conversion and church membership	1960	18	82
Converting a married woman	1960	19	86
Conversion without marriage	1960	20	87
Questionable conversion	1963	15	78
Miscegenation & conversion of Negroes	1963	16	83
Unprovable claims to conversion	1963	17	87
Laymen conducting a conversion	1969	25	96
Converting a Gentile mother whose children remain Christian	1969	29	110
Changing the surname of a convert	1971	27	154
The reverting proselyte	1971	28	159
Our attitude towards apostates	1971	30	169
Dubious conversion	1974	30	136
Converts and the rabbi's responsibility	1977	14	66
Questions concerning proselytes	1980	17	72
Incomplete conversion	1980	18	75
Gerut and the question of belief	1983	65	209
Conversion w/o formal instruction	1983	66	211
Mental competency of a convert	1983	67	215
Convert w/a Christian family	1983	70	240
An apostate proselyte	1983	71	241

B. CIRCUMCISION

Title	VOL.	ENTRY #	PAGE #
Circumcising the son of a Gentile wife	1963	21	99
Circumcision for children of mixed marriage	1971	29	165
Circumcision of proselytes	1977	15	71
Circumcision of adult proselytes	1983	68	216
Prospective convert who fears circumcision	1983	69	268

C. MARRIAGE

Title	VOL.	ENTRY #	PAGE #
Cohen marrying daughter of mixed marriage	1963	34	158
Mixed marriage on Temple premises	1971	19	108
Apostate wedding attendance	1980	43	189
Status of children (marriage)	1983	145	441
Reform Judaism and mixed marriage	1983	146	445
Prayer for couple contemplating inter-marriage	1983	147	465

	VOL.	ENTRY #	PAGE #
Rabbi officiating at a mixed marriage	1983	148	466
Rabbi officiating at a mixed marriage	1983	149	467
Marriage with a "Messianic Jew"	1983	150	471
Non-Jewish clergy participating in a wedding with a rabbi	1983	151	474

D. CHILDREN

	VOL.	ENTRY #	PAGE #
Baptism of a child before adoption by a Jewish couple	1963	20	97
Circumcizing son of a Gentile wife	1963	21	99
Status of apostate's children and adults	1963	26	120
Gentile stepfather at a Bar Mitzvah	1969	23	91
Naming a child after a Gentile grandparent	1971	23	134
The pregnant proselyte	1971	25	143
Reform and mamzerus	1980	Inq.5	256
Children of mixed marriages	1983	60	193
Status of children of doubtful religious background	1983	61	195
Status of a Gentile-born child adopted into a Jewish family	1983	62	199
Report of the committee on Patrilineal descent on the status of children of mixed marriages	1983	Appendix	547

E. DEATH & BURIAL

	VOL.	ENTRY #	PAGE #
Burial of an apostate	1963	27	127
Kaddish for apostates & Gentiles	1963	28	132
Burial of non-Jews in Jewish cemetery	1969	39	154
Convert buried in Christian cemetery	1974	33	151
Convert and Jewish burial	1974	54	240
Disinternment of a Jew from a Jewish cemetery for reburial in a Christian cemetery	1977	38	179
Gentile's burial in a Jewish cemetery	1980	21	88
Rabbis officiating at a funeral of a Jew in a non-Jewish ceremony	1983	93	312
Rabbi officiating at Christian Scientist's funeral	1983	94	314
Burial of prospective convert	1983	97	321
Burial of non-Jewish wives in Jewish cemeteries	1983	98	323
Non-Jewish burial in a Jewish cemetery	1983	99	335
A proselyte reciting Kaddish for deceased parents	1983	123	386
Kaddish for a Unitarian sister	1983	124	387
Memorializing Christian relatives	1983	125	390

F. SYNAGOGUE & MISC.	VOL.	ENTRY #	PAGE #
Who is a Jew	1963	14	73
Pre-converts participating in services	1969	22	88
Gentile membership in synagogue	1977	47	221
Gentile president for sisterhood	1977	53	249
Gentile's part in the Sabbath service	1980	07	33
Participation of non-Jews in a Jewish public service	1983	06	21
Synagogue membership of a mixed couple	1983	10	45

G. INDEX BY VOLUME

Reform Responsa, 1960
#18, 19, 20, 46

Recent Reform Responsa, 1963
#12, 14, 15, 17, 20, 21, 26, 27, 28, 34

Current Reform Responsa, 1969
#22, 23, 25, 29, 39

Modern Reform Responsa, 1971
#19, 23, 25, 26, 27, 28, 29, 30

Contemporary Reform Responsa, 1974
#30, 33, 54

Reform Responsa for our Time, 1977
#14, 15, 38, 47, 53

New Reform Responsa, 1980
#07, 17, 18, 21, 43, Inquiry #05

American Reform Responsa, 1983
#6, 10, 60, 61, 62, 65-71, 93, 94, 97-99, 123-125, 145-151, Appendix

APPENDIX IV

WHAT IS OUTREACH?

Outreach is a program which aims to:

* Welcome those who seek to investigate Judaism;

* Welcome Jews-by-Choice as full citizens of the Jewish community;

* Welcome intermarried couples into the congregation. Outreach seeks to enable non-Jewish partners to explore, study and understand Judaism, thereby providing an atmosphere of support in which a comfortable relationship with Judaism can be fostered;

* Educate and sensitize the Jewish community to be receptive to new Jews-by-Choice and intermarried couples;

* Encourage people to make Jewish choices in their lives through community support, adult education and availability of Jewish resources;

* Assist young people in strengthening their Jewish identity and in examining the implications of interdating and intermarriage for themselves.

There is a national UAHC/CCAR Commission on Reform Jewish Outreach. Each UAHC Regional Office has an Outreach Coordinator on staff. In addition, many congregations have Outreach Committees.

WHAT IS THE HISTORY OF THE OUTREACH PROGRAM?

On December 2, 1978, Rabbi Alexander Schindler, President of the Union of American Hebrew Congregations, called upon the Board of Trustees to establish a program of Outreach which would develop responses to the needs of individuals converting to Judaism, intermarried couples, children of intermarriages and those interested in learning about Judaism. The UAHC Trustees unanimously adopted a resolution calling for the study and development of a program of Reform Jewish Outreach and endorsed the creation of a Joint Task Force with the Central Conference of American Rabbis. David Belin was named Chairman and Rabbi Max Shapiro Co-Chairman, followed by Rabbi Sheldon Zimmerman. This Task Force presented a report to the 1981 UAHC General Assembly, which then adopted five resolutions calling for a comprehensive program of Reform Jewish Outreach.

(For a detailed report of the Task Force, see "A Summary of the Report of the UAHC/CCAR Joint Task Force on Reform Jewish Outreach," August 1981.)

In 1983, the Task Force became a Joint UAHC/CCAR Commission on Reform Jewish Outreach with a mandate to develop programming, resources and materials for the various Outreach target populations. Lydia Kukoff was named Commission Director, David Belin continued as Chairman, and Rabbi Steven Foster was named Co-Chairman. In 1988, Mel Merians was named Chairman, and Rabbi Leslie Gutterman was named Co-Chairman.

WHERE IS OUTREACH TODAY?

The program has expanded and currently includes programming for:

* Intermarried couples and couples contemplating intermarriage
* Children of intermarried couples
* Jews-by-Choice
* Those interested in choosing Judaism
* Parents of intermarried couples
* Inreach to born Jews on issues relating to Jewish identity and attitudes toward the changing Jewish community

The Outreach Staff currently includes an Associate Director, Dru Greenwood, as well as Sherri Alper, Consultant for Special Programming, and Outreach Coordinators in every UAHC region. Coordinators serve as resources for congregations in their regions, working closely with professional staff and Outreach committees to design and implement a suitable Outreach program for each congregation. Coordinators also administer regional and sub-regional programs such as Introduction to Judaism, "Times and Seasons," and various follow-up programs for intermarried couples and Jews-by-Choice.

WHAT PROGRAMS DOES OUTREACH OFFER FOR INTERMARRIED COUPLES AND COUPLES CONTEMPLATING INTERMARRIAGE?

"Times and Seasons: A Jewish Perspective for Intermarried Couples" is a program which was created in response to the needs of the intermarried, to serve as the critical first step taken by unaffiliated intermarried couples seeking to explore Judaism in the context of differences in their backgrounds.

This eight-week discussion group is designed to clarify the Jewish partner's feelings about Judaism and to provide the non-Jewish partner with a greater understanding of Judaism and the Jewish community. The group facilitator is a trained professional. Relevant personal issues discussed include: religious involvement while growing up, the religious and cultural issues each partner confronts in the relationship with the other and with extended family, holiday celebrations, and each couple's concerns about the religious identity of their children.

Although the program is offered from a Jewish perspective, there is no attempt to convert the non-Jewish partner. The program, however, helps participants to articulate the differences between Judaism and Christianity. We believe that understanding these differences will allow fuller communication between partners and a more secure base for decision-making for the couple. Facilitators have been trained by the UAHC to lead these groups. A complete guide to the program, <u>Times and Seasons: A Jewish Perspective for Intermarried Couples - A Guide for Facilitators</u>, is available from the UAHC Press.

In addition to the "Times and Seasons" programs, many congregations offer a variety of programs for intermarried couples and their children. Sample programs are presented in <u>Reform Jewish Outreach: The Idea Book</u>.

WHAT PROGRAMS DOES OUTREACH OFFER FOR THE JEWISH PARENTS OF INTERMARRIED COUPLES?

Jewish parents of intermarried couples, or couples contemplating intermarriage, are one of the most accessible Outreach populations. Yet these parents often report feeling isolated within the very community that they have been a part of for so long.

The goals of the discussion groups for parents are:

* To provide participants with a non-judgmental, supportive setting in which they can meet with others sharing similar concerns;

* To provide participants with an opportunity to discuss the impact of their child's interfaith relationship on their family and to develop constructive responses to various family dilemmas that arise;

* To communicate the philosophy and objectives of Reform Jewish Outreach;

* To acquaint participants with existing Outreach programs in their own community;

* To provide participants with the clear message that the Reform Jewish community seeks to continue to reach out to them, their children and their grandchildren.

These groups are led by trained facilitators, many of whom have been trained at regional training sessions. A complete guide to the program, <u>Jewish Parents of Intermarried Couples: A Guide for Facilitators</u>, is available from the UAHC Press.

WHAT PROGRAMS DOES OUTREACH OFFER FOR THOSE CONTEMPLATING CONVERSION TO JUDAISM AS WELL AS FOR THOSE WHO ARE INTERESTED IN LEARNING MORE ABOUT JUDAISM?

Introduction to Judaism classes are offered on both the community and congregational levels. The main focus of the 12-18 week class is basic Judaism, including holidays, life cycle events, history, theology and Hebrew. Students learn what it means to live a Jewish life and how to begin to practice Judaism. This program may include a psycho-social component which deals with the personal implications of choosing Judaism. Post-introduction programs and various workshops and discussion groups are also offered. One of our hopes is that participants in these groups will integrate fully into temple life and take advantage of the many educational, social and worship opportunities in their own temples.

Some congregations offer a series of programs designed to help the new Jew-by-Choice become integrated into the Jewish community. These programs often include discussion groups, workshops, study sessions and <u>Shabbatonim</u>. Program ideas may be found in <u>The Idea Book</u>.

WHAT PROGRAM HAS OUTREACH CREATED TO ASSIST RELIGIOUS SCHOOL TEACHERS, CANTORS, AND RABBIS IN DEVELOPING A SENSITIVITY TO THE NEEDS OF CHILDREN WHO HAVE NON-JEWISH RELATIVES?

The William and Frances Schuster <u>Guidelines for Outreach Education</u> reflect the cooperative effort of the UAHC Department for Religious Education and the Joint Commission on Outreach. The <u>Guidelines</u> contain three basic sections:

1) A statement of background and goals;

2) A faculty workshop to:

   * Provide background information about Reform Jewish Outreach,

   * Articulate some of the needs of children who have non-Jewish relatives,

   * Through values clarification exercises, help congregational and professional leadership clarify their own feelings regarding Outreach-related issues and policies,

   * Explore scenarios and strategies for dealing with various related situations which arise in the classroom;

3) A suggested approach to dealing with Outreach-related issues through the religious school curriculum.

Currently, the regional Outreach staff and the Department for Religious Education staff are available to assist with the faculty workshop. Training relating to classroom management and curriculum is handled by the Department for Religious Education, while the psychosocial component is handled by the Outreach staff.

WHAT PROGRAMS DOES OUTREACH OFFER FOR REFORM JEWISH YOUTH?

One of our goals is to assist young people in examining the implications of interdating and intermarriage for themselves as well as for the future of the Jewish people. We encourage our youth to explore and strengthen their Jewish identity.

A number of programs have been created for use in a variety of settings. Several of them are highlighted in The Idea Book and Reaching Adolescents: Interdating, Intermarriage and Jewish Identity.

HOW DOES OUTREACH PREPARE CLERGY, EDUCATORS, MENTAL HEALTH PROFESSIONALS AND LAY LEADERS TO WORK WITH THE VARIOUS OUTREACH POPULATIONS?

Facilitator training sessions for "Times and Seasons" and groups for the Jewish parents of intermarried couples are held on a regional basis. During the past few years, professional development courses have been offered through HUC-JIR to prepare clergy for meeting the changing needs of the Jewish community. HUC-JIR students also participate in special one-day Outreach seminars. An intensive one-week Outreach internship, hosted by Temple Emanuel in Denver, Colorado, provides students with an opportunity to experience and learn about the implementation of Outreach programs on a congregational level.

The Commission on Outreach offers on a regular basis workshops and presentations at various professional conferences, e.g. Central Conference of American Rabbis (CCAR), American Conference of Cantors (ACC), Coalition for the Advancement of Jewish Education (CAJE), and the American Psychological Association (APA). We also work closely with the CCAR Committee on Gerut.

Defining the Role of the Non-Jew in the Synagogue: A Resource for Congregations encourages the development of a response which reflects sensitivity to those non-Jews who have made a commitment to raising their children as Jews while seeking to preserve the integrity of Judaism.

HOW IS OUTREACH INVOLVED IN INREACH?

The ultimate goal of the Outreach program is to strengthen Judaism by helping individuals build their personal connectedness to Reform Judaism. We seek to assist born Jews and Jews-by-Choice in developing and enhancing their Jewish identity. The success of Outreach is dependent upon our ability to strengthen the bonds between members of the Jewish community and those who have chosen to associate with the community. These bonds are strengthened when every individual has a clear sense of his or her religious and ethnic identity. Outreach is not only about conversion and intermarriage. It is about being Jewish. Outreach enables us to look inward at who we are as Reform Jews and outward toward our changing community. Awareness of each enriches the other. A valuable resource which enables congregations to explore the relationship between Outreach and Inreach is **Outreach and the Changing Reform Jewish Community: Creating An Agenda for Our Future - A Program Guide**.

APPENDIX V

SUGGESTED READING

UAHC OUTREACH PUBLICATIONS

Program Guides:

Defining the Role of the Non-Jew in the Synagogue: A Resource for Congregations

Introduction to Judaism: A Course Outline compiled and edited by Stephen J. Einstein and Lydia Kukoff (2 volumes: Instructor's Guide and Student's Resource Book)

Jewish Parents of Intermarried Couples: A Guide for Facilitators

Outreach and the Changing Reform Jewish Community: Creating an Agenda for Our Future

Reaching Adolescents: Interdating, Intermarriage and Jewish Identity

Reform Jewish Outreach: The Idea Book

Times and Seasons: A Jewish Perspective for Intermarried Couples -A Guide for Facilitators

To See the World Through Jewish Eyes: Guidelines for Outreach Education: Developing Sensitivity to the Needs of Children Who Have Non-Jewish Relatives (A volume of the UAHC William and Frances Schuster Curriculum)

Books:

Every Person's Guide to Judaism by Stephen J. Einstein and Lydia Kukoff

The Jewish Home: A Guide for Jewish Living by Daniel B. Syme

Jews and Non-Jews: Getting Married by Sanford Seltzer

New Jews: The Dynamics of Conversion by Steven Huberman

Why Choose Judaism: New Dimensions of Jewish Outreach by David Belin

Your Jewish Lexicon by Edith Samuel

Note: Unless indicated otherwise, the above program guides and books are available through the UAHC Press, 838 Fifth Avenue, New York, NY 10021, (212)249-0100.

Films:

<u>Choosing Judaism: Some Personal Perspectives</u> (A Video Cassette) with Lydia Kukoff (Available from the UAHC TV and Film Institute)

<u>Intermarriage: When Love Meets Tradition</u> Produced by Lydia Kukoff; directed by Ilana Bar-Din (Available in both 16 mm and 1/2" VHS at special low rates to UAHC congregations. Order films directly from Direct Cinema Limited, P.O. Box 69799, Los Angeles, CA 90069, or call (213) 653-8000.)

ADDITIONAL PUBLICATIONS

<u>A Guide to Interfaith Marriage: But How Will You Raise Your Children</u>? Steven Carr Reuben. Pocket Books, NY, 1987.

<u>The Intermarriage Handbook: A Guide for Jews and Christians</u>. Judy Petsonk and Jim Remsen. Arbor House/William Morrow, NY, 1988.

<u>Mixed Blessings: Marriage Between Jews and Christians</u>. Paul and Rachel Cowan. Doubleday, NY, 1987.

<u>122 Clues for Jews Whose Children Intermarry</u>. Sidney and Betty Jacobs. Jacobs Ladder Publications, Culver City, CA, 1988.

<u>Clues about Jews for People Who Aren't</u>. Sidney and Betty Jacobs. Jacobs Ladder Publications, Culver City, CA, 1985.

<u>The Jewish Experiential Handbook: The Quest for Jewish Identity</u>. Bernard Reisman. Ktav, NY, 1979.

APPENDIX VI

OUTREACH STAFF

Lydia Kukoff, Director
Dru Greenwood, Associate Director
Rabbi Renni Altman, Director
Programs for the Unaffiliated
Sherri Alper, Consultant for Special Programming

Union of American Hebrew Congregations
838 Fifth Avenue
New York, NY 10021

Canadian Council
Jessie Caryll
CCLC
1520 Steeles Ave. West
Concord, Ontario
Canada L4K 2P7
(416) 660-4666

Great Lakes Council/Chicago Federation
Mimi Dunitz
UAHC
100 W. Monroe St.
Chicago, IL 60603
(312) 782-1477

Mid-Atlantic Council
Elizabeth (Robin) Farquhar
61 G Street SW
Washington, D.C. 20024
(202) 488-7429

Midwest Council
Marsha Luhrs
UAHC
10425 Old Olive Street Road
Suite 205
St. Louis, MO 63141
(314) 997-7566

New Jersey/West Hudson Valley Council
Kathryn Kahn
UAHC
1 Kalisa Way
Suite 104
Paramus, NJ 07652
(201) 599-0080

New York Federation of Reform Synagogues
Ellyn Geller
UAHC
838 Fifth Avenue
New York, NY 10021
(212) 249-0100

Northeast Council
Paula Brody
UAHC
1330 Beacon St.
Suite 355
Brookline, MA 02146
(617) 277-1655

Northeast Lakes Council
Nancy Gad-Harf
6361 Timberwood South
West Bloomfield, MI 48322
(313) 788-0827

Northern California Council
Pacific Northwest Council
Lisa Cohen Bennett
UAHC
703 Market St.
Suite 1300
San Francisco, CA 94103
(415) 392-7080

Pacific Southwest Council
Arlene Chernow
UAHC
6300 Wilshire Blvd.
Suite 1475
Los Angeles, CA 90048
(213) 653-9962

Pennsylvania Council/
Philadelphia Federation
Linda Steigman
UAHC
2111 Architects Building
117 S. 17th St.
Philadelphia, PA 19103
(215) 563-8183

Southwest Council
Debby Stein
12700 Hillcrest Road
Suite 180
Dallas, Texas 75230
(214) 960-6641

Southeast Council/
South Florida Federation
Rabbi Rachel Hertzman
UAHC
Doral Executive Office Park
3785 N. W. 82nd Avenue
Suite 210
Miami, FL 33166
(305) 592-4792